Greetings
Bro Wilson & Sis Vallorie,
May God's Richest
Blessings Be Always
yours!

Blessings & Prayers

Bishop Jimmie R. Horton

Live The Unlimited Life

Jimmie R. Horton

WESTBOW
PRESS
A DIVISION OF THOMAS NELSON
& ZONDERVAN

Copyright © 2014 Jimmie R. Horton.

All rights reserved. No part of this book may be used or reproduced by any means, graphic, electronic, or mechanical, including photocopying, recording, taping or by any information storage retrieval system without the written permission of the publisher except in the case of brief quotations embodied in critical articles and reviews.

WestBow Press books may be ordered through booksellers or by contacting:

WestBow Press
A Division of Thomas Nelson & Zondervan
1663 Liberty Drive
Bloomington, IN 47403
www.westbowpress.com
1 (866) 928-1240

Because of the dynamic nature of the Internet, any web addresses or links contained in this book may have changed since publication and may no longer be valid. The views expressed in this work are solely those of the author and do not necessarily reflect the views of the publisher, and the publisher hereby disclaims any responsibility for them.

Scripture taken from the King James Version of the Bible.

Photo courtesy of Jimmie R. Horton's files.

Any people depicted in stock imagery provided by Thinkstock are models, and such images are being used for illustrative purposes only. Certain stock imagery © Thinkstock.

ISBN: 978-1-4908-2298-3 (sc)
ISBN: 978-1-4908-2297-6 (hc)
ISBN: 978-1-4908-2299-0 (e)
Library of Congress Control Number: 2014901425

Printed in the United States of America.

WestBow Press rev. date: 4/1/2014

I dedicate this book to my lovely wife, Michelle, who enormously encouraged and sacrificially supported me in many ways. I also dedicate this book to my dear children, Faith, Avery, Jimmie Jr., and Hannah, and all of my grandchildren. I am most grateful to my illustrious parents, Rev. Joshua and Mother Mattie Horton. This dedication is also to my beloved siblings, my beloved church family at Gospel Mission Temple, and to all our generations hereafter.

This book is also dedicated to all of my readers. Be inspired, and be blessed!

Bishop Jimmie & Mrs Michelle Horton,

Thank you for helping to make our world better.

Joy!

Maya Angelou

July 22, 2011

Above is a personally autographed greeting from Maya Angelou to Bishop Jimmie and Michelle Horton

Contents

Preface ix
Acknowledgments xi
Introduction xiii
1. Unlimit Yourself 1
2. Know from Whence You Have Come 17
3. The Old Folks 29
4. Spiritual Giants 41
5. A Courageous Journey 47
6. Chosen to Answer the Call 55
7. The Highest Quality of Life 71
8. Born to Be Significant 81
9. Hope for Marvelous Change 99
10. Live Your Life by Faith 109
11. Faith Cometh by Hearing 125
12. Know Your Purpose in Life 133
13. Purpose Is Spiritual 143
14. Purpose Is about People 151
15. Don't Major in the Minors 175

16. A Powerful Relationship with God 195
17. Love Thy Neighbor 209
18. Trust in God's Unlimited Ability 235
19. The Christ-Centered Life 241
20. The Abundant Blessings of Forgiveness 249
21. Take Control of Your Fivefold Health 255
22. God Has Great Plans for Your Success 259
23. Unlimit Your Mental Boundaries 263
24. Let Excellence Be Your Goal 269
25. Enjoy Every Stage of Your Life 275
26. Prayer Is a Powerful Privilege 283
27. Always Put God First 289
28. Rejoice Even in Tough Times 295
29. Respect and Be Respected 299
30. Be Blessed by Humility 303
31. Accept What God Allows 307
32. Be Thankful Every Day 313
33. The Enormous Power of Praise 317
34. The Endless Value of Wisdom 321
35. Your Integrity Is Priceless 325
36. The Fullness of God's Love 329
37. A Lot of Living to Do 335
Special Memorial Tribute to My Father 341
Works Cited 343

Preface

Have you ever stopped to evaluate the quality of your life? Today you can move toward the next level of enjoying your highest level of living. Life is more than existing. We merely exist when we live our lives without definition and divine purpose. To live life with definite purpose is life at its best. Life is at its best when it is lived with the faith and the great expectations that bring us to our destiny of all that we were meant to be and all that we were predestined to experience.

Acknowledgments

Those to whom I am enormously grateful are too numerous to mention, as I acknowledge the overwhelming supporters who made this book a reality.

First and most ultimately, I am grateful to God, as He has been my greatest inspirer, advisor, and editor.

I give special acknowledgements to my enthusiastic secretarial staff: Mrs. Joy Johnson, Mrs. Annie Pickett, Mrs. Barbara Daniels, Ms. Patty Gibbs, Ms. Kathy Wogomon, Ms. Janelle Vanerstrom, Ms. LaBridgette Tensley, Ms. Debbie Teague, Ms. Monica Johnson, Mrs. Martha Spears and Ms. Sasha Trice. I am also thankful to my spiritual mentors who have ministered to me untiringly, many of whom have gone on to be with the Lord.

I would like to thank my dear friend, Dr. Maya Angelou, who inspired me in many ways during the completion of this publication. After learning about our church, she called and said, "Bishop Horton, only God can grow a church as great as Gospel Mission Temple." I will always treasure her autographed book and her handwritten greeting that read, "Bishop and Mrs. Horton, thank you for helping to make our world better. Joy!" I will always treasure the delightful conversations Dr. Maya Angelou and I shared by phone.

Introduction

This book was written out of my strong passion to inspire, encourage, and convince others to believe that God can provide enormous and endless benefits to all who choose to live their lives victoriously, beyond all possible limitations.

I often encourage my family, friends, and even myself to tap into God's immeasurable opportunities of life. I think all of us at some time have been tempted to underestimate our abilities, prospects, and possibilities. I am strongly convinced that every human being can be a success story in spite of all possible defeats in the past, present, and future. We are all faced with challenges every day, and we must make daily choices that will assure victory and triumph in all circumstances and situations. These choices are made by faith giving birth to positive attitudes and optimistic behavior. When we stand on the promises of God, we can reverse every negative encounter we may face in our future.

We can learn to have marvelous faith in place of our shallow doubts and fears. We can experience prosperity in all of our impoverished circumstances. We can have total victory in the midst of all adversity. My faith in the power of the almightiness of God has caused the level of my hope to be exceedingly multiplied. I am strongly convinced that life can be very good, even in times that seem hopeless. In spite of what I have seen with my eyes, my faith in God always gives me a brighter outlook on life. We all must confess that we have human limitations. Some of us are naturally smarter, wiser, and more intelligent than others. However, I am more than sure we can rise beyond our natural ability and experience life at a supernatural level of potential and prosperity.

I am very impressed with a quote from Tony Dungy, a Super Bowl-winning coach, who said in his book, *Quiet Strength*, "Don't get me wrong—football is great. It's provided a living and a passion for me for decades. It was the first job I ever had that actually got me excited about heading to work. But football is just a game. It's not family. It is not a way of life. It does not provide any sort of intrinsic meaning. It's just football. It lasts for three hours and when the game is over, it's over."

I emphatically agree with Tony Dungy. Life itself must go on after the game is over. With this thought in mind, we should be concerned with the big picture of life. We should focus on the total sum of life and not be distracted by one fascinating feature. God is concerned about all of our accomplishments. He does not want us to experience partial victory. He wants us to succeed in every endeavor and become high achievers.

On our road to success, we may have had some experiences that have the appearance of failure, but these encounters are part of God's success plan. For instance, when Joseph was put into the pit by his own brothers, it was the first step that would lead him to his noble state in the palace in Egypt. Life is full of pitfalls, but for those of us who believe in Christ, we can rise above them and triumph over the lows in life. We were all born in the pits of sin, but as David said, "He took my feet out of a horrible pit, out of the miry clay, and set them on a rock and established my going" (Psalm 40:2).

Jesus is the perfect model of success. He was successful in everything He did while on the earth. In spite of the gruesomeness of His crucifixion, death, and burial, His resurrection can be classified as the greatest and most profound revolution in the history of mankind. In the midst of our pain and sorrow, we should be encouraged to bear them with joy when we look at the example of how Christ triumphed through the greatest of pain and sorrow. He showed us how we can bear our grief and disappointments, both courageously and victoriously.

I am persuaded to believe that the longer we live this life, the better we should be at living it. Divine provision has already been made that all of our faults and failures may be transformed into amazing victories. We have all made mistakes. I have learned how to profit from my mistakes by allowing them to be stepping-stones toward positive change. There is hope for all of our unrighteousness. We should not be afraid to deal with our human deficiencies. We can improve our future by keeping before us the caution of never repeating the disappointments of our past.

The optimism that accompanies our faith can miraculously overshadow the doom and gloom of our past, present, and future. This faith will elevate our attitude, and our attitude will elevate our altitude, causing us to believe that our best is yet to come, and tomorrow will be by far brighter than today.

Remember, your victory is already won. It is left up to you to live the lifestyle that accompanies your destiny. "For those whom God foreknew, He also predestined to everlasting abundance and everlasting success" (Romans 8:29). Your success happens the very moment you begin to believe. The manifestation of your success happens with the process of effort, patience, and perseverance. With patience and determination, your faith will assure that the process is already accomplished!

1

Unlimit Yourself

I can do all things through Christ, who gives me the strength.
Philippians 4:13

Life is a gigantic proposition! It is a multifaceted undertaking that should be dealt with very seriously. Too often, we identify ourselves with only one part of the whole essence of life. You can experience a prosperous and successful life in spite of the conflicts of your past and the adversities of your future. You can absolutely succeed against all odds. Today is your opportunity for a new beginning on the road to personal success.

You are God's choice. You may be overlooked by some and rejected by others, but your time has come. Today is your day to confess your significance as one of God's special creations, with a bright forecast for the future. Remember, there is no confidence greater than the confidence that is produced by believing the Word of God. Feed your faith with a daily reminder of who you are, whose you are, and the remarkable person you are becoming. Your significance is not of your own credibility, but you have been pronounced to the royalty of the Most High God by the Almighty God Himself. For the mouth of the Lord has spoken it!

You are God's plan; you are God's best plan. He desires the best for you so much that He is willing and able to absolutely reverse those unfavorable things that have happened to you. Every human being is a special creation that God Himself has created for a unique and divine purpose. He has made it possible for each of us to experience the abundant life, regardless of all physical, social, economic, intellectual, or spiritual challenges, barriers, and limitations.

I was born Black. I was born economically poor. I was born in the state of Mississippi. However, I was rich in the things that mattered most. I was destined to be successful and prosperous in spite of the biased stereotypes associated with these statistics. The prejudices that were associated with these stereotypes stigmatized Blacks who were born in the South during the time when the horrible Jim Crow laws were very prevalent.

I was born in 1949, the seventh of twelve children, to the Reverend Joshua Horton and Mattie Horton, during the heat of America's oppression of people of color. My parents moved to Jackson, Mississippi, from the small rural town of Edwards, Mississippi, about a decade before my birth. I can still vividly recall where my small and humble beginnings took place.

Our house was a "shotgun house" at 223 Clifton Street near the heart of downtown Jackson. Shotgun houses were houses that you could see straight through from the front door to the back door. They resembled looking down the barrel of a shotgun. There were only three bedrooms, a bathroom, and a kitchen. Some of the happiest days of my childhood were spent at this house.

The love and strong family structure created by my parents greatly compensated for our limited income and economic status. We never thought of ourselves as poor. We only knew we had less than some and more than others in the neighborhood. I remember how diverse our neighborhood was. Our father and mother were very well respected because of their reputation of having strong Christian values.

I can recall the many unforgettable neighbors on Clifton Street. I remember Miss Hattie and Miss Emma Palmer, who were high-class socialite ladies. These two sisters lived in a big beautiful house, which symbolized wealth and dignity for Black people of that era. Miss Emma taught at the neighborhood elementary school where my sisters and brothers attended. They represented a stately lifestyle that all of the neighbors admired.

Many times, Miss Emma Palmer would give my sister Ann a note to take home to Mom, requesting Ann to assist her mother while Miss Palmer was away. Ann enjoyed the dignified company that often visited their home. Their high-class dating and entertainment was so refined that it was uniquely impressive. My sister Ann found their sophisticated laughter and singing around the piano to be very intriguing. The Palmer sisters made such a great impression upon us that now, even well into my adulthood, I ask my sister Ann to tell me more about Miss Emma and Miss Hattie Palmer. Although my parents were not as educated as the Palmer sisters, Miss Emma and Miss Hattie, like the other affluent Blacks, included Mom and Dad in their social circle.

There was another family known as the Tobias family. They, like our family, were well respected. The Tobias family was well mannered, and we always got along well together. Many summer evenings, the Horton children had a lot of fun playing in the alley with the Tobias children until sundown. Larry Tobias and my brother Eddie often caught and sold roaches to Mr. Barlow, who owned the bait and fisherman shop around the corner from our house. Larry and Eddie would buy pop, cookies, peanuts and candy and share it with us.

All of the Clifton Street neighbors gave my dad the respect of an esteemed minister. My parents were known as "the church-going husband and wife with all those children." There were others in our neighborhood not as fortunate, such as Ms. Bernice and Mr. Elick. They fought and argued often and lived in what we called "the Alley." My older sisters and brothers told me that Ms. Bernice and Mr. Elick would always fight on Friday evenings after Mr. Elick received his paycheck.

We resided in several homes after Clifton Street, but the most prominent of all of our residences was the big white house at 1412 Hill Street. This house was located near Jackson State University in a section of town called Washington Addition, which was first known as the Gowdy Community. I was about six years old when we moved into this house. I remember how excited we were about the big white bathtub that had running water. It was by far better than the round tin tub that we had to pour water into on Clifton Street. This house also had a dining room, which was quite a step up from the shotgun house.

This neighborhood consisted of people who were thought of as more prominent and productive. Our next-door neighbors were the Reverend Abraham Davis and Mrs. Bonnie Bell Davis. They had two sons, Lewis and Lawrence, and two daughters, Lois and Zanette. The two daughters were closer to my age. We developed a close friendship that remains very special, even to this day.

Across the street from our house was a little grocery store where I worked after school. The owners were Mr. John Henry and Mrs. Agnes Allen. They paid me two dollars a week to do odd jobs around the store. I saved those two dollars every week and bought my first bicycle from the Firestone Company for thirty-eight dollars.

Growing up as a Horton was a very special experience. We received most of our prominent spiritual, educational, and social influences as children while living on Hill Street. We attended the Third Temple Church located at 1405 Morehouse Street, and on the third Sunday in December 1959, I publically confessed Christ and joined the church. The pastor was the Honorable Reverend Joe Ezra Bearden. The Third Temple Church played a vital part in nurturing and molding my positive self-image.

I later became a Sunday school teacher, a junior deacon, and an assistant Sunday school superintendent. I enjoyed my involvement in the youth department in every way. At the age of fifteen, I began taking piano lessons and within one year, I was playing hymns well enough to play for the junior choir. I later became one of the prominent musicians of the church and was chosen to work with various programs during the holidays and for other special events. We often joined with other churches for youth activities. I became deeply involved in the district, state, and national convention of our church.

Our parents encouraged us to participate in church, school, and community activities. My father taught nightly Bible classes in our home, and we often reviewed the Sunday school lesson after our evening meal. Sometimes he would be too long-winded, and we felt he was overdoing it. We desired to be like many of our neighborhood friends, who were still outside after sundown, having fun. However, I always enjoyed hearing the Word of God.

My siblings and I highly valued our parents' fireside teachings. Mom always supported Dad in enforcing rules; even those we thought were too strict. When someone misbehaved, she would often say to us, "I am going to tell your dad when he gets home." Those were some powerful words that immediately reformed our behavior. Both of my parents were powerful and positive role models. Their influences made permanent, life-changing differences in our lives, even to this day.

As I stated earlier, Dad was the stronger disciplinarian, but Mother did her share to discipline us. Dad and Mom believed in the Scripture, "If you spare the rod, you will spoil the child" (Proverbs 13:24). As a result, none of us was spoiled by them.

Dad would always counsel us before any form of spanking. Mom, on the other hand, would counsel while she was spanking us. This form of discipline yielded great dividends in all of our lives. At that time, we thought they were mean, but now we know it was their way of demonstrating their great love for us. Good parents never neglect to correct their children through proper discipline.

My older brothers were living on their own by the time our family moved to Hill Street. The Hill Street house accommodated all of us quite comfortably. My siblings, Joshua Jr., Arthur, Annie, Isabella, Eddie, Dorothy, Lindsey, Mattie, Roy, David, and Barbara, made the atmosphere very exciting and adventurous. There was never a dull moment. Momma was the best mom a mother could ever be. I often refer to her as the "Miracle Worker." Just as Jesus took the two fish and five loaves of bread and fed the mass of five thousand people, Mother always found a way to take what we had and make it go a long way.

My brother Lindsey and I were very close as we grew up together in the Hill Street neighborhood. Lindsey was two years younger than I. He was my boyhood buddy. We enjoyed the homemade kites we made from newspapers, sticks, and glue, which was made from flour and water. We created our own toys, such as go-carts and scooters. We enjoyed rolling car tires, playing baseball, and building tree houses.

Lindsey and I made extra money by selling pop bottles. Our sister Dorothy Jean would sometimes accompany us. Jean and I were also very close. She joined us as we gathered pop bottles to sell. We spent our money on candy bars, ice cream, pop, and big boxes of freshly baked cookies. We bought these goodies at a thrift bakery known as the Dixie Cookie Company. We paid only a dime for a big box of freshly baked but broken cookies.

I shall always treasure the summer nights when we would sit out on the front porch and play a game called My Car. We had two teams, each representing a different direction. Every time a car would come from the north side of the street, team one would get a point. When a car would come from the south side of the street, team two would get a point. After a certain period, the number of cars was tallied, and the team with the most cars would win.

We would also enjoy catching fireflies (lightning bugs) and putting them in jars. It was an awesome delight to see this lantern-like light glowing in the dark.

We would also play a game called Rocking Teacher. The person with the rock would represent the teacher. The teacher would have a rock in his closed fist and put it behind his back. Then, putting both fists in front of the children, each child was given the chance to guess which hand held the rock. The child who earned the most points would then become the teacher. These were simple but most enjoyable children games.

One of our favorite games was hide-and-seek. One of

the children would chant while the others would hide. The caller would cover his face and chant:

> "Last night, night before,
> Twenty-four robbers at my door.
> I got up, let them in,
> Hit 'em in the head with a rolling pin.
> All hid, say knee-high,
> All around my base, ain't got no hundred."

After this chant, those who were hidden came out and tried to touch the base before the caller could catch them. Our fun was very simple.

On summer days, you could hear the girls playing hopscotch, jump rope, and ring games like Little Sally Walker. You could hear them singing:

> "Little Sally Walker,
> Sitting in a saucer,
> Rise Sally rise,
> Wipe your weeping eyes,
> Put your hand on your hip,
> Let your backbone slip.
> Ah, shake it to the east,
> Ah, shake it to the west,
> Ah, shake it to the one that you love the best."

You could also hear the girls jumping rope and singing,

> "Miss Mary Mack, Mack, Mack
> All dressed in black, black, black,
> With silver buttons, buttons, buttons,
> All down her back, back, back.
> I asked my momma, momma, momma,
> For fifteen cents, cents, cents,
> To see the elephant, elephant, elephant,
> Jump the fence, fence, fence.
> He jumped so high, high, high,
> He touched the sky, sky, sky,
> He never came back, back, back,
> 'Til the Fourth of July, 'ly, 'ly."

The boys could be heard playing my favorite game, baseball. I loved baseball. We did not have a baseball diamond so we created our diamond in the center of the block, right in front of our house. There were enough Horton children to make up our own baseball team. I always enjoyed being the coach and the owner of the ball and bat, which gave me some prestige. Besides the Horton children, other children on our block played on our team, including Winston Gale, Junebug Henderson, Catherine Henderson, Billy Gale, Gregory Anderson, Jennifer Gale,

Brenda Gale, Dot Redmond, and Barbara Redmond. We also enjoyed playing tag-football and marbles.

The fun of those good ol' days of my childhood surpasses explanation. It is amazing the creative, free fun that we had, compared to most of the games children play today. In those days, most of our games required physical activity, in contrast to today's expensive computer games.

I was greatly inspired to become a schoolteacher by a gentleman named Mr. Johnny W. Jones. He was the superintendent of our Sunday school and taught sixth grade at my elementary school, Isabel Elementary, in Jackson, Mississippi. I was highly impressed by his intellect and spiritual mannerism. Mr. Jones modeled the image that affected the inspirational choices I made as a lad of twelve years old in becoming a schoolteacher and preacher. I am convinced those choices were preordained before my birth. I must also mention my third-grade teacher, Mrs. Amnease T. Heard. She played a profound part in my becoming a successful educator, as I will mention later in this book.

I graduated from Jim Hill High School in May 1968 and entered Jackson State College in the fall of that year. Jim Hill High School and Isabel Elementary School gave me a very solid educational foundation. I was highly respected by all of my teachers and fellow students. I was elected class chaplain of my senior class at Jim Hill.

Before going to Jackson College, I had the remarkable experience of spending two summers at Tougaloo College in the Upward Bound program. I was elected student president of this college preparatory program in 1967. Those summers at Tougaloo College were remarkable and unforgettable. I met friends locally, nationally, and abroad. We all got along like brothers and sisters.

Dr. Naomi Townsend, the director of this program, took a very special interest in me. She often gave me leadership roles in student activities. I was called upon to play the piano for several music groups while at Tougaloo College. I had many outstanding teachers of diverse backgrounds, and I was exposed to some of the highest levels of the fine arts in literature, music, and drama.

One of my most outstanding teachers was Sister Mary Lenore, a Catholic nun of the Order of Saint Benedict from Eau Claire, Wisconsin. She gave me private piano lessons without cost. Being reared in the state of Mississippi, I found it unusual that a White teacher would be so interested in teaching a young man of color. Many years after leaving Tougaloo, Sister Mary Lenore continued to show a special interest in me. When she became aware that my brother Eddie was a soldier in Korea, she asked for his address and sent him a big box of delicious food. My brother so vividly remembers and fondly speaks of her to this day. Much of Sister Mary Lenore's music was willed to me as she approached her death. She remains one of my most unforgettable mentors.

After leaving Tougaloo, I was fortunate to receive a four-year scholarship, including all paid books, through the Thirteen-College Curriculum Program. Mrs. Luana Clayton was the director of this program. She had such a great impact on my life, and I made a connection with her many years after she retired. We remained close until she went home to glory. Momma Clayton made a beautiful quilt for my wife and me, which we will always treasure in her memory. Her husband, Mr. Hugh Clayton, was my counselor for two summers at Tougaloo College in the Upward Bound program. He and I also were very fond of each other. Their daughters, Melissa and Jean, also became dear friends.

I highly appreciate the important work ethic that both of my parents instilled in me. From my elementary school days to the present, I have valued the benefits of hard work and a very busy, constructive life. In high school, I worked at a printing shop during the summer and as a paperboy year-round.

During the summer of 1966, while in the tenth grade at Jim Hill High School, I became employed at McDonald's restaurant. While working at McDonald's, I experienced some very harsh discrimination and racism. I was limited to working only in the back of the restaurant as a janitor and maintenance worker, which included keeping the parking lot clean and washing the dishes. Only the White men and women were allowed to be cashiers. I remember how I would pray silently as I burned inside with disgust and disappointment toward this unjust system.

I remember a White boy named Dennis who was very unkind to me. I shall never forget the strength I displayed and how I would not retaliate when he provoked me to anger. I always went home at night, full of hope and assurance, knowing that there was a brighter day ahead. I did not accept this unfair and demeaning system. I had faith that the evils and unfair treatment of the Black race would eventually change. I knew that somehow God would position me to make a powerful and indelible difference so that I could bring remarkable social and spiritual change. The horrible experiences I endured at McDonald's did not diminish my good and healthy self-image. I was strengthened by these adversities.

As years passed, I rehearsed in my mind the inequitable employment principles of McDonald's. I feel very proud that in spite of these hardships, the powerful teachings of my parents kept me looking forward to better things in life.

Today, I am very pleased when I return to Jackson and see that Blacks are not only working as cashiers and managers of McDonald's, but they are owners of franchises all over the United States. This was the fulfillment of that hope I felt as a young man in the summers of 1966 and 1967.

We were taught as children never to think we were less than anyone, regardless of how others may perceive us. I felt I was just as good as any of those White boys. In fact, I thought they needed some of the qualities of my character and God-given favor. We were also taught that God created from one blood all nations of mankind. Our parents taught us that the power of love is, by far, greater than the power of hate and that Black racism is just as detrimental as White racism. We should never try to overcome evil with evil, but we should overcome evil with good.

2

Know from Whence You Have Come

*That the generation to come should arise
and declare them to the next generation.*
Psalm 78:6

Our strong and rich spiritual heritage goes back to the legacy of my paternal grandfather and grandmother, the Reverend Morris Horton and Emily (Tyner) Horton. They were sharecroppers in Edwards, Mississippi. Sharecroppers were Black people who were victimized by what I would call another form of slavery.

White plantation owners took advantage of many Blacks in the South. They were told they would receive a certain amount of money at harvest time if they picked a specific amount of cotton. Some of the plantation owners would have the same sad story at the end the harvest: "We broke even again." There were those who even falsely implied that the laborers were in debt to them. This was to say that there was no money owed to the sharecroppers at the end of the season. At the end of the harvest, these plantation workers were just as impoverished as they were the year before.

Papa and Mama Horton were not victimized by this system because of their special favor and unfaltering faith in their God. They remained full of integrity as they embraced their God and family with love, in spite of all adverse circumstances. As a result of this, they never went to bed hungry. They instilled in their children strong work ethics and the hope that a brighter day was ahead. They demonstrated the good life that accompanies the old-time religion.

Papa Morris Horton was born in Edwards, Mississippi, in 1880 to Anthony and Rilla Horton and passed away in October 1967. Mama Emily Horton was born in Edwards, Mississippi, in 1883 to Richard and Ella Brow-Tyner and passed away in April 1951. Their seven children were Anna, Carrie, Morris, Isabella, Joshua, Estella, and Sherman. Their twins, Lazarus and Martha, died shortly after birth.

The rich and noble legacy of my maternal grandparents has enormously blessed me. My mother's father, Ed Lloyd, was born to Ed and Amanda Lloyd on July 4, 1872, and passed away on February 23, 1943. Annie Lloyd was born to Wilson and Mary Allen on August 4, 1875, and passed away on January 9, 1972. They were more fortunate than most of the other Blacks in Edwards, Mississippi. Papa Eddie Lloyd was the son of a wealthy White plantation owner, who willed him over two hundred acres of land. During this era, Blacks very rarely owned this amount of land.

My grandparents' children were Lucille, Charlie, Amanda, Cedella, Maybelle, Annie Bea, Nelson, Gus, Alex, Chester, and Mattie. They all lived to adulthood and told their stories of struggle, survival, and strength.

It is essential that the generations hereafter know the profound stories of the trials, tribulations, and triumphs of the past. My son Jimmie Jr. gives his own personal account in his own words:

In keeping with the tradition of my family's rich heritage, my father's phenomenal positive life experience has greatly motivated me to become the man that I am and will be. My paternal grandfather positively influenced him. My grandfather's existence was superbly enriched by the Christian life of his father, who was also a gospel preacher.

Along with having a lineage of strong male role models, the loving hands of powerful females have nurtured and shaped my life. In our home, we have a picture of my paternal great-great-grandmother, who was born a slave in 1848. She was a deeply religious woman who passed her Christian heritage on to the generation that followed.

In my father's adolescence, he could always be seen sitting under the holly tree at Isabel Elementary School during recess, silently reading his King James Bible. He was an example of the kind of lad who went against the flow of the world; he was the kind of man who possessed great leadership qualities, which were enveloped in love and concern for others. He was always seeking the perfect will of God in his life.

My father lived with his parents and eleven brothers and sisters in West Jackson, Mississippi. One day after coming home from Isabel Elementary School, his teacher came to his home to complain about my father's strong religious convictions. She told his parents that he was too serious about God and that he read his Bible when he should have been playing. She also mentioned he did not participate in dancing because he thought it was "worldly." My father told his parents that the teacher was playing sensual music for the class to dance to and that he knew fifth graders shouldn't be dancing to such. He knew that he would get into trouble for not participating and that his peers would jeer at him, but his principles and self-respect were more valuable to him.

My father is not a stranger to opposition. He was often ostracized by his fellow classmates and called "preacher boy," "square," and "old sanctified." They didn't know that whenever he heard these encouraging words, his faith in God increased more and more. He knew that it was an honor to be called a preacher, to be called an inspiration, to be referred to as sanctified, and to be called square. A square doesn't roll when the wind blows; it stands firm and hold its ground, and all of its angles are right. He equated himself with Samuel, one of the greatest biblical patriarchs who ever lived and who was called to be a preacher when he was a boy. To be sanctified is to be set apart for God's use.

My father constructed tools of determination and perseverance out of his childhood experiences with poverty and opposition. Growing up during the time of segregation in the South, he was a student at Jackson State University when a mob of policemen poured gunfire into Alexander Hall and massacred a fellow Jacksonian. My father was one of the students who marched against the indecencies of racism and segregation. But more than that, he was the kind of youth who always stood up for what was right, no matter the cost.

With the help of God, these utensils enabled him to become the first college graduate in the history of our family. He was not satisfied with just being a college graduate; he kept on going to school until he received his master's degree in guidance and counseling. He became one of the greatest educators the Davenport Public School System has ever known.

After teaching for a period of twelve years, he formally heeded the call to the ministry. With the help of my mother and two of his brothers and their wives, he organized a church in the lower level of his split-foyer home. He named the church Gospel Mission Temple. It took only one year for the congregation to outgrow our home. The flock moved to a large community center for worship. After being there for four years, Gospel Mission Temple purchased a beautiful turn-of-the-century church with beautiful stained-glass windows. Nine years later, under the guidance of my father, the congregation was able to purchase thirty-five acres of prime land, well within Davenport's city limits. Construction of an elegant, three-million-dollar church building for Gospel Mission Temple began immediately and was finished in the year 2001. With added construction, it is now valued at ten million dollars. It is one of the largest growing congregations in Iowa. My father still holds fast his strong conviction that segregation is wrong. The church consists of many people of various age groups and races and cultural, ethnic, and social backgrounds.

From the story of my father's life, I have learned many principles that I have found to be beneficial to my life. With the aid of compelling motivation, one possesses the ability to thrive, despite unfavorable circumstances. Throughout my years of schooling, all of my abilities and discipline have been dedicated to learning and achieving. My academic record and involvement in numerous activities are witness to that dedication. I have maintained a cumulative 4.0 GPA. Of a class of four hundred, along with five of my classmates, I received academic excellence, numerous scholarships, and awards.

However, I have learned that my desire to achieve academically shouldn't surpass my efforts to help others. I have displayed the desire to serve others by engaging in several charitable events, and I have been involved with many organizations that have promoted them. I have been a Genesis Medical Center venturing volunteer, a member of the Local School Advisory Committee, an ACE Big Brother Big Sister activities organizer, and a volunteer Voters News Service reporter for ABC, AP, NBC, CBS, and FOX. I am a member of my church's prison ministry, brotherhood organization, and youth ministry. I am also a church organist, and I play for the youth choir, the mass choir, and the praise team. One of my most memorable acts of service was the labor and toil I endured to help the building process of my church's new edifice on North Pine Street. This dedication has been rewarded with many academic triumphs and recognitions, including earning three awards for academic excellence and receiving the

News Channel 4 Community Leadership award. From my father's life story, I have learned to assume an active role in society that will allow me to make perpetual and limitless deeds of service.

My aspirations to become a doctor of medicine are also influenced by my father's life and by the principle that says personal achievement shouldn't exceed the desire and ambition to serve others. The vision of having the role of a doctor is also motivated by the enjoyable thought of being a lifetime student. I understand that there are many new discoveries in medical science and more efficient technologies that are developed every year, such as the gamma knife. I am amazed at the perfection and complexity of the human body, including the many processes that are carried out through numerous systems, working to maintain a level of homeostasis. I am delighted at the idea of physically enhancing the quality and duration of many lives. Life cannot possibly be lived to its highest level of productivity, performance, or pleasure if it's ceaselessly invaded with illness. Every time I see an operation, I recognize it as something beautiful, an effort to promote the life of another being, to free it from the bondage, suffering, and frustration that accompany illness by assisting the process of healing. This profession has many benefits: continuous learning, constant challenges, and the satisfaction of having the opportunity to pry at the hands of Death until he loosens his grip on my patient.

My father is truly a man with a vision, someone who has held fast to his convictions and dreams, enabling him to forge ahead and make those dreams come true. My goals are also attainable, as long as I keep them alive through my actions. I believe my past success is an indication of my future success, and the benefactors of my dreams are unrestricted, not being refused because of color, creed, or economic circumstances. I am confident that my visions, which have been influenced by my father's story, are dreams that are attainable, as his were, and are not illogical hallucinations.

Jimmie Horton Family Genealogy

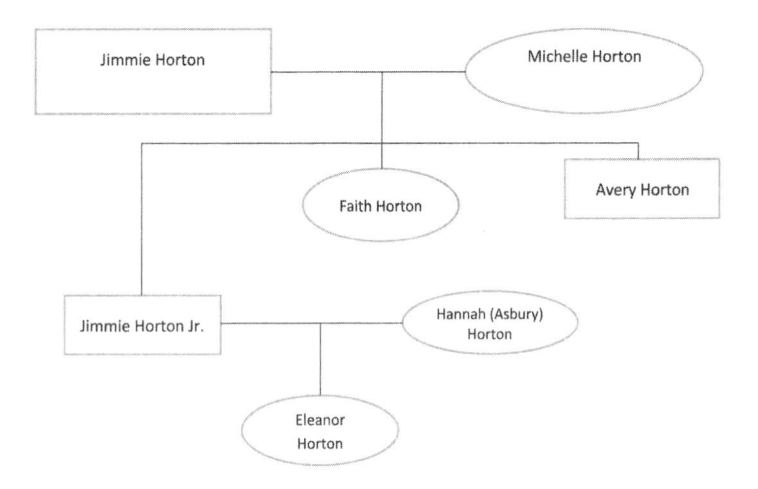

- Jimmie Horton — Michelle Horton
  - Faith Horton
  - Avery Horton
  - Jimmie Horton Jr. — Hannah (Asbury) Horton
    - Eleanor Horton

Horton Paternal Genealogy

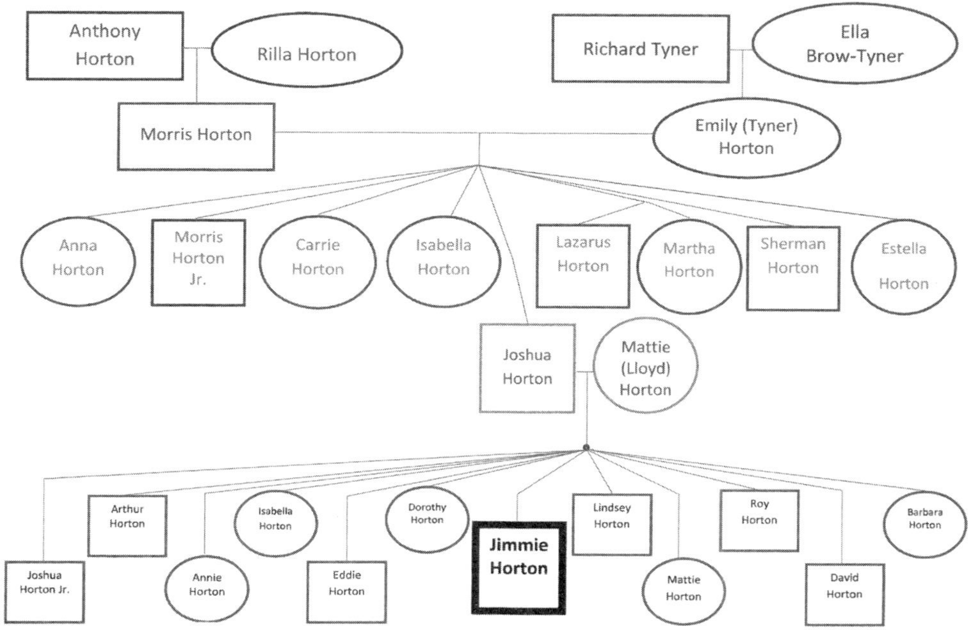

- Anthony Horton + Rilla Horton
  - Morris Horton + Emily (Tyner) Horton
    - Anna Horton
    - Morris Horton Jr.
    - Carrie Horton
    - Isabella Horton
    - Lazarus Horton
    - Martha Horton
    - Sherman Horton
    - Estella Horton
    - Joshua Horton + Mattie (Lloyd) Horton
      - Joshua Horton Jr.
      - Arthur Horton
      - Annie Horton
      - Isabella Horton
      - Eddie Horton
      - Dorothy Horton
      - **Jimmie Horton**
      - Lindsey Horton
      - Mattie Horton
      - Roy Horton
      - David Horton
      - Barbara Horton
- Richard Tyner + Ella Brow-Tyner
  - Emily (Tyner) Horton

Horton Maternal Genealogy

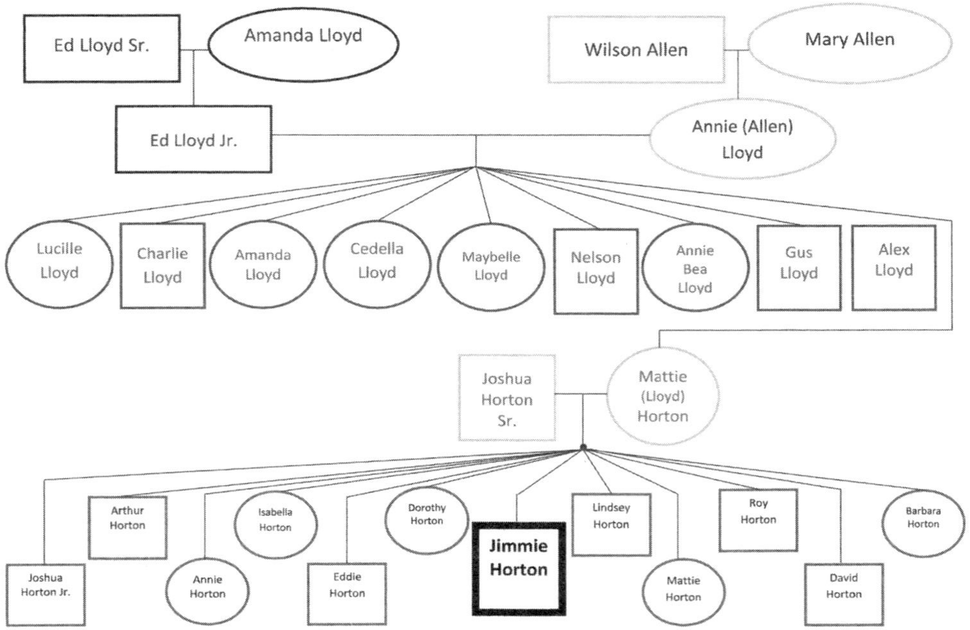

- Ed Lloyd Sr. — Amanda Lloyd
  - Ed Lloyd Jr.
    - Lucille Lloyd
    - Charlie Lloyd
    - Amanda Lloyd
    - Cedella Lloyd
    - Maybelle Lloyd
    - Nelson Lloyd
    - Annie Bea Lloyd
    - Gus Lloyd
    - Alex Lloyd
  - Annie (Allen) Lloyd — Wilson Allen
    - Mary Allen

- Joshua Horton Sr. — Mattie (Lloyd) Horton
  - Joshua Horton Jr.
  - Arthur Horton
  - Annie Horton
  - Isabella Horton
  - Eddie Horton
  - Dorothy Horton
  - Jimmie Horton
  - Lindsey Horton
  - Mattie Horton
  - Roy Horton
  - David Horton
  - Barbara Horton

3

The Old Folks

Hold fast to the traditions which you have heard from the elders.
2 Thessalonians 2:15

I was greatly influenced by the "old folks" of our neighborhood, church, and community. It was the old folks who would often say to me, "Boy, one of these days you gonna be somebody." I always enjoyed hearing those words. In fact, I already thought I was somebody who was becoming a better somebody. The old folks consistently confirmed my inner perception of my valuable self-worth. I have never thought of myself as a proud or arrogant person, but I have always known I was special. This assurance caused me to develop into an individual of wholesome and healthy confidence. I spent much of my time with children of my own age, but the old folks always had a special place in my heart and were a joy to be around.

I can never say enough about the old folks of my family and our neighborhood community. Mr. Jerry Hollins was one of my most favorite of the old folks. My brother Lindsey and I were his errand boys and visited him nearly every day after school. The errands we made to the grocery store and to the ice house supplied us with the nickels and dimes we needed to buy our daily Baby Ruth candy bar, pop, Moon Pies, and cookies.

Mr. Jerry Hollins never called me by my name. He always referred to me as "mah boy" and treated me like I was his son. He owned a big house without any electricity or gas. He cooked on an old, wooden stove and burned kerosene lamps for light. I remember the big pecan tree in his backyard. He often allowed us to pick pecans, and he would reward us by giving us half of all that we gathered. Looking back in retrospect, Mr. Jerry Hollins was one of my first employers. The importance of the old work ethic was transferred as a personal value at this stage of my early youth. I must mention our youth choir director, Mrs. Lula Shirley. She was a very polished and dignified old lady who was a choral music perfectionist. She would always say to us, "We will not sing this song until it is per-fec-ted."

One day she gave me one of my greatest and most profound lessons in the use of good grammar. I was riding in the car with her and other youth choir members as we were on our way to sing at a local church service. Mrs. Shirley was as quiet as a mouse until one of the choir members told me of the good time he had at an event on the day before. I responded by saying, "I wish I had went!" With a loud and sophisticated voice, Sister Shirley corrected me by saying, "You mean you wish you had *gone*!" For the remainder of that trip, I remained in total silence. From that day to this one, I have been most sensitive to using proper grammar at all times. After that experience, Sister Shirley and I often went to the church to practice our favorite songs together. This made me feel very special. Even now, I can hear her as I accompanied her on the piano, singing one of her old favorite spirituals:

Talking 'bout a child that do love Jesus,
Here is one, here is one.
Talking 'bout a child that do love Jesus
Here is one.
Talking 'bout a child whose bound for glory,
Here is one, here is one.
Talking 'bout a child whose bound for glory,
Here is one.
Ever since I heard the gospel story,
I've been traveling up the path to glory.
Talking 'bout a child who do love Jesus,
Here is one.

My first lesson in financial management and investment was given to me by a dear old lady in our neighborhood, Mrs. Allie D. Roundtree. She gave me a piggy bank that was half full of nickels, dimes, and quarters. I shall never forget her kind words of wisdom that have profited me even unto this day. She said, "Now, son, take this bank and fill it up, and save it for a rainy day. Remember that in life, the amount you save is more important than what you spend. Don't spend it all; learn to save."

Mrs. Ruth Cook-Sanders, along with her daughter, Mary Lou, gave me the honor of being staff musician for the Cook Funeral Home. This position gave me access to meeting and interacting with a large population of the community and individuals from all over Mississippi. To them, I will always be grateful.

Every summer our family was blessed with a visit from my dad's sisters, Aunt Estella and Aunt Sugar Bea, who lived in Chicago. They were two of the most devout Christian women I have ever known. Some of my most valuable family history was acquired through my interaction with them during their visits to Jackson and my trips to Chicago.

Whenever they came to visit, they usually stayed with Aunt Anna. My aunts always inquired about how my siblings and me were doing in school and church as well as our goals and aspirations in life. They would take time to listen to each of us respond. They brought excitement when visiting and made all of us children feel very special.

During my high school days, I spent several nights a week with Aunt Anna, who was a very lonely widow. Aunt Estella, while visiting Aunt Anna, would often give her emotional testimony. The atmosphere of the house glowed with the radiance of their joyful singing and praising the Lord.

Aunt Estella will always be remembered for the exciting way she told her testimony of divine healing of terminal cancer. After her doctor told her that there was no hope, she was miraculously healed, because she asked the Lord to do for her what He had done for the prophet Hezekiah. She lived to be almost ninety years old, with a powerful testimony and a victorious life.

Aunt Bea, who was an Apostolic woman, was very excited about telling us about receiving the baptism in the Holy Ghost. She would often say to us, "If you don't have the Holy Ghost, you must have it." She once told one of my sisters, "Daughter, the Lord can fill you right there where you are sitting." At that point, Aunt Bea became overwhelmed with an ecstatic shout that was so impressive that those who did not have the Holy Ghost became strongly interested in receiving it.

Aunt Bea and many of the old folks believed in the full gospel, which includes the baptism in the Holy Ghost. I, like the spirit-filled pioneers, am convinced that being filled with the Holy Ghost is mandatory to the Word of God. Everyone should have this experience in order to grow into the fullness of the promise that Jesus made. It can be explained as a precious gift of the Spirit and as a second act of grace, which is subsequent to salvation.

In Acts 1:8, Jesus said, "You will receive power after the Holy Ghost has come upon you." Another supporting Scripture is in Matthew 3:11, where the disciple John said, "I indeed baptize you with water, but He that comes after me is mightier than I. He shall baptize you with the Holy Ghost and with fire."

I must substantiate these Scriptures with the admirable words of the Apostle Paul as he passed through the upper coast of Ephesus. He asked certain disciples, "Have you received the Holy Ghost since you believed?" They responded, "We have not so much as heard whether there be any such thing as the Holy Ghost" (Acts 19:2). Then Paul prayed for them, and they received the baptism in the Holy Ghost.

I will always remember an old sainted lady, whom we referred to as Miss Jessie Stamps. She was a very devout Christian lady. Miss Stamps was known all over the neighborhood for her special love of children. She invited us to her house and would teach us Bible lessons. I remember those hot summer nights, when she could be heard picking her guitar and singing:

Do Lord
Do Lord, O do Lord, do remember me,
Do Lord, O do Lord, do remember me,
Do Lord, O do Lord, do remember me,
Do remember me.

Take Me Through
Take me through, dear Lord, take me through,
Take me through, dear Lord, take me through,
Take me through, dear Lord, take me through,
And I'll do what you want me to do.

To My Father's House
Come and go with me,
To my father's house,
To my father's house,
To my father's house,
Come and go with me,
To my father's house,
There is joy, joy, joy.

Her most favorite song was "What Kind of Man Jesus Is," written by Aaron Neville. She would go on to sing:

Ananias, Ananias,
Tell me what kind of man my Jesus is,
He walked the sea, He raised the dead,
Tell me what kind of man my Jesus is.

Miss Jessie Stamps had the persona of someone who stepped right out of the Bible into modern times. One day, she and her visiting friend from Dallas, Texas, whom she so affectionately called Sister Sheriff, prayed for me. They wore dresses that were as white as snow. I was only a boy, barely ten years old, but I was as serious as a grown man about my salvation. These sainted women's prayers will never be forgotten as long as I live.

I remember another sainted mother who was known all over the community as Mother Ethel Drake. She was a powerful woman of unusual spiritual conviction. She always wore long dresses and would consistently pray all through the day. Every time I visited her, she would insist that I get down on my knees and pray with her. We prayed for hours. Being just a little boy, I would always be very tired when leaving her house. I would always leave, saying I would not come back anytime soon, but I would find myself coming back the next day. She told me that

God had a special calling on my life. I visited her from the time of my boyhood until she went to be with the Lord.

After moving to Davenport, Iowa, in 1972, I fellowshipped with the Mount Olive Church of God in Christ and was pastored by another of my fathers in the gospel, the Right Reverend William Henry Frison. He and his lovely wife, Missionary Helen Frison, with an unfeigned love, loved me as their very own son. Pastor Frison grew to be close to my brothers and me. He performed our weddings and often gave us good spiritual advice. His dear wife and I often reminisce about the wonderful things he did to touch the lives of many. His memory shall continue to live on in our thoughts.

It was my golden pleasure to meet, at the Mount Olive Church of God in Christ, a very sainted mother, Mother Julia Howard. She was a precious woman of God. She often reminded me of the time when one of my coworkers in the school system told her about the young man who just moved into town to teach in the Davenport schools. She was told by this individual that I acted like a preacher. Her response to that statement was, "Bring him to us." I will never forget how Mother Julia and her husband, Papa Herman, included me as part of their family. They will always have a special place in my heart. I am so happy Mother Julia and Papa Herman lived to see their prophecy upon my ministry come to pass.

I became very fond of all the members of the congregation at Mount Olive Church, but the old folks impressed me the most. Mother Myrtle Carter would cook delicious meals and invite my brother Eddie and me over for dinner. She would cook her delicious, fried chicken, mashed potatoes and gravy, green beans, collard greens, and potato pie. She was a great inspiration in many ways to my brothers and me, whom she called the "Hardan" brothers.

My life has also been touched by great social and civic activists among the old folks, such as Mrs. Cecile Cooper. She was militant, with a strong passion to fight for equal rights for minorities in the Quad Cities. Her home was often a meeting place for civil rights activists of various races, where they would assess the progress of the Civil Rights Movement. Mrs. Cooper was a very personal friend to my brother Eddie and me. She introduced us to many distinguished local and national leaders who shared her passion to make an indelible mark on social and spiritual change in our city and nation. She was one of the founders of many organizations that also shared this passion, such as the Negro Heritage Society and the Freedom Riders against the Jim Crow laws in the South.

I will always treasure the memories of Mother Rosa Lee McGee, one of my most unforgettable spiritual matriarchs. She was a very powerful prayer warrior, who is now 109 years old. Mother McGee is an excellent example of living the unlimited life. Her life portrays this through her longevity of years and through her great and prosperous journey of walking with God. Her devout faith is highly remarkable. She has often said to me, "Son, even if there were no heaven, just living on earth for Jesus is more than worth it all."

Mother McGee spent most of her life in Jackson, Mississippi. As a young, beautiful Black woman, she often passed for being White. She would travel across the country, attending church conventions and revivals. Those with whom she traveled would often send her into the "*White only*" restaurants to buy food. I am sure Mother McGee was thinking, *I become all things to all people that I may win others.* We always found this quite humorous.

Mother Matilda Bingham was a special, spiritual woman of profound faith and prayer. I shall always remember her gentle and godly way of encouraging and inspiring all with whom she came in contact. She had a strong faith in the power of prayer. Mother Bingham's daughter, Mary Lee Francis, has often mentioned how her mother would come into their bedrooms at night when they were children and check on them. As she went from room to room, she would lay her hands on them and whisper a prayer. I will always treasure her godly wisdom and precious memory.

Another one of the renowned matriarchs of latter-day Christendom is Mother Fannie Gant. She possessed qualities that are a true reflection of a godly woman. She lived the eloquent life that reflected love, wisdom, and Christ-like compassion for every man, woman, boy, and girl. It was during my high school years that she encouraged me with love super-extraordinary. She was a very stately woman who could walk with kings and queens but not lose the common touch.

May the wisdom of these trailblazers continually multiply through their daring and courageous contributions. And may the "old folks" and "spiritual giants" of all of our generations be forever memorialized and treasured. May their memory live long, and may the prosperity of their labor be transferred into the essence of our future. We shall never forget their legacy or their endless contributions of labor and love. We shall forever treasure their memory, and we dare not ever forget the urgency of their silent voices echoing to us, "Carry on ... carry on ... carry on."

4

Spiritual Giants

Continue in the things which you have learned knowing of whom you have learned them.
2 Timothy 3:14

My life has been touched by many spiritual giants, both men and women. Many of them I have known personally through interaction and relationships. I have learned of others through my extensive reading and research, which has blessed me with a wealth of knowledge of great men and women of renown religious, social, civic, and intellectual contributions to Christendom. It is very obvious that these militant men and women have had radical experiences with God. I have been enormously touched and blessed by their super-extraordinary examples.

The greatest spiritual influences in my life were my

own dear parents, the Right Reverend Joshua and Mother Mattie Horton. Another was Bishop Charles Price Jones, who was the founder of the Christ of Christ Holiness, USA, and a renowned hymn writer. Bishop Charles Price Jones also was cofounder of the Church of God in Christ along with Bishop Charles Harrison Mason. Bishop Mason and Bishop Jones were two of the most militant holiness preachers of all time. I must also mention the Reverend Joe Ezra Bearden, my first pastor; Dr. Marcus Butler, one of my dear friends and mentors who founded of the Amazing Church of God in Christ; and Bishop Major R. Conic, the first successor of Bishop Charles Price Jones.

Others who indelibly influenced my life were the illustrious Bishop Obadiah Wesley McInnis, who ordained me as Elder and Pastor of Gospel Mission Temple on September 29, 1984, in Detroit Michigan. It was very fitting that we chose Bishop McInnis as the dedicatorial speaker of the first church edifice on Fourth Street. God had profoundly used him and his dear wife to lay the foundation for this great ministry. We shall always honor their great contributions to our ministry. His wife, "Dear," often encouraged my wife as a young pastor's wife. We will always treasure his prolific wisdom and sermon that inspired us the most, "Fear Not Little Flock, for It Is God's Good Pleasure to Give to You the Kingdom." Another father in the gospel, Apostle Lobias Murray, man of God extraordinaire, who consecrated me to the office of Bishop in July 2004 in Dallas, Texas. Words cannot express the impact this great spiritual giant left upon my life and ministry. His militant stand against unrighteousness was super-extraordinary. Apostle Lobias Murray and his dear wife, Dr. Evangelist Shirley Murray, founders of Full Gospel Holy Temple Incorporate, are two outstanding influences in my life.

My passion as an activist for civil rights, social equality, and justice has been greatly influenced by the Reverend Dr. Martin Luther King Jr. My life has been impacted by patriarchs of early religious reform, such as John and Charles Wesley, who were early pioneers of the Methodist Movement. I have also been deeply touched by the noble legacy of the great founder and reformer of Protestantism, Martin Luther. Another one of the most outstanding religious patriarchs in America and founder of the African Methodist Episcopal Church is the great pulpiteer and religious statesman Bishop Richard Allen. My life has also been impacted by the world-renowned Evangelist Billy Graham, who has spread the gospel to millions around the world.

The history of the Christian Church in America has been enriched by the life and legacy of the great catalyst and founder of the Pentecostal movement worldwide, Bishop William Seymour. He conducted the first renowned

Pentecostal revival, known as the Azusa Street Revival, which took place in Los Angeles, California, from 1906 to 1909. Bishop Seymour was a powerfully militant Black preacher, who has been honored with the esteemed title of the Father of Pentecost. His Azusa Street Revival of 1906 gave birth to over five hundred million Pentecostals and innumerable others of the Christian faith worldwide.

I must also mention Bishop Garfield T. Haywood, founder of the Apostolic Oneness Movement known as the Pentecostal Assemblies of the World. Bishop Haywood inspired Bishop Robert C. Lawson to be the prolific founder of the Church of Our Lord Jesus of the Apostolic Faith. Bishop Haywood and Bishop Lawson were very militant statesman of the Apostolic doctrine. Both of them greatly influenced Bishop William Bonner, who is the presiding bishop of the Church of Our Lord Jesus.

Some of the most profound encouragers to me as a pastor are the Honorable Bishop Arthur M. Brazier, Bishop Gilbert Earl Patterson, Bishop and Mother Hurley Bassett, Bishop and Mrs. Bennett Wolfe, Bishop Herman Murray, Bishop Larry Keil, Bishop Paul Cannon, and the Board of Bishops of the Full Gospel Holy Temple Inc. They all have inspired me significantly.

Bishop and Sister Bennett Wolfe played an exceptional part in supporting my wife and me from the inception of our ministry. I have often reminded them of how they did not wait until God blessed us as remarkably as He has before they decided to befriend and wholeheartedly support us. To them, we will always be grateful. They proved not only to be our sister and brother in the Lord but some of the dearest friends.

Likewise, Bishop and Mother Hurley Bassett have made outstanding contributions of encouragement to Gospel Mission Temple. We will never forget the many years they made their annual visit to our church to inspire and encourage us along the way.

Bishop Maurice Bingham of Jackson, Mississippi, encouraged me as I was growing up at Third Temple Church. He, along with the counseling staff at Jackson State University, enhanced my aspiration to become a certified counselor. Bishop Bingham gave me my first counseling job at Camp Pioneer when I was a junior at Jim Hill High School, I went on to pursue a master's degree in guidance and counseling, which has been very profitable to my ministry and my interactions with the young people in the public school system.

One of God's most honorable spiritual giants, Elder John Gordon, has supported us through his many spiritual gifts. Through his powerful gift of evangelism, he has blessed my ministry enormously for many years. I must also mention my beloved brothers, who have been most loyal to my ministry: Elder Eddie Horton, Elder Roy

Horton, Elder David Horton, Chief Lindsey Horton, and Elder Arthur Horton. As I think of all of those who have touched my life, such as my Sunday school teachers, vacation Bible school teachers, public school teachers, and mentors, there are too many names to mention. As the old African proverb goes, "It takes a village to raise a child." I am grateful to say that my spiritual village consisted of great men and women who have left a monumental and indelible impact on my life and ministry.

5

A Courageous Journey

*Be courageous and I will make your journey
prosperous and successful.*
Joshua 1:7–8

In May 1972, I graduated from Jackson State College with a bachelor of science degree in education, and I applied for a teaching position in the Jackson Public Schools. Opportunities for new teachers at that time in Jackson were very limited. After much prayer, I applied for a teaching position in the Davenport Community School District in Davenport, Iowa. I was recommended for this teaching position by one of my classmates from college and was hired immediately. This was divine intervention. I had never even heard of Davenport, Iowa. In fact, my pronunciation at that time was "Davenport, *Ioway*."

I left for Davenport on Sunday, August 20, 1972,

to teach fifth grade at Lincoln Elementary School. I remember how happy I was, although I also experienced mixed emotions, because it was hard to leave my family, who was so special and dear to me. My oldest sister, Ann, purchased my ticket and gave me spending money. I arrived at the Jackson airport with my small blue suitcase, my Bible, and about a hundred dollars. I shall never forget how my little sister Barbara cried. I consoled her by telling her that I would come back to see her often. A smile swept her face when I told her I would also send her toys. The smile on her face made my departure so much easier. Barbara and I are still close, and I will always treasure my relationship with her and her lovely family.

I will never forget that Sunday evening when the Delta flight landed at O'Hare Airport. I went to the information desk and asked about my connecting flight. I approached the attendant and asked, "Will you please tell me where I connect with Air Ioway?" The gentleman kindly replied, "Do you mean Air I-O-WA?" I thanked him and since that day, it has become a part of me to pronounce "Iowa" with a Midwestern accent.

The plane was an old, small, shabby commuter plane. My thirty-five-minute flight to Moline, Illinois, was quite daring but adventurous. I was so happy to finally arrive at Quad City Airport. I still treasure the little blue suitcase, which will always be the reminder of my humble beginnings in Davenport.

Mr. Tom Smith, the principal of Lincoln Elementary School, had informed me that when I arrived at Quad City Airport, a man by the name of Mr. Esterbrook would be awaiting my arrival at the airport. Mr. Esterbrook cordially greeted and welcomed me, with Iowa hospitality.

My first night in Davenport was spent in the home of Willie and Ethelene Owens, who treated me like a relative. The next day, I found a nice efficiency apartment at 930 Perry Street. The little room had a small refrigerator, a small stove, and a couch that converted to my bed at night. I borrowed money that same week from the Davenport Teachers Credit Union and purchased a black-and-white television. I had enough money for food to last until I received my first paycheck.

My apartment was just around the corner from Palmer College of Chiropractic. I lived on the corner of Tenth Avenue and Perry Street. The college atmosphere was tranquil, simple, and sophisticated. It is amazing how quickly I adjusted to my new environment. There was a little neighborhood grocery store called Omar's Royal Blue, around the corner from my small efficiency apartment on Brady Street. My refrigerator could only hold very little, so I bought my groceries day by day as I needed them. I learned how to cook. I only had one plate, a fork, a spoon, a knife, a pot, and a little skillet.

I often walked downtown, which was a few blocks from my house, to eat out at the famous Bishop's Buffet. I managed very well without a car because Lincoln School was just a few blocks from my apartment. The church I attended was only a few blocks away as well. Everything I needed was within walking distance, which was the same blessing I was accustomed to back home in Jackson, Mississippi. It was surprising how quickly I became accustomed to the Iowa snow. Mississippi winters were mild, but Iowa winters were cold and snowy, yet beautiful.

Many of my weekends were spent in Chicago, where I visited the home of my Aunt Estella, Aunt Bea, Aunt Carrie, Uncle Sherman, and my cousins, Ivory Anderson, Randolph Anderson, Barbara Lee, and their children. They showed me so much love. I matured quite a bit during this time of my sudden independence.

Mr. Tom Smith, the principal of Lincoln Elementary School, grew to be very fond of me. He was very professional and kind. He was the first Black administrator in the Davenport Community School District. Mr. Smith happened to live in the same apartment complex where I resided.

Teaching at Lincoln Elementary School was a great

challenge indeed, but it was also very rewarding. I was only twenty-three years old, and I was given the responsibility of teaching twenty-seven students. Most of these students were from low socio-economic backgrounds. Many of them had already been stigmatized by former teachers as problematic or troublemakers. I became very emotionally attached to every one of them and even to this day, I can recall each of their names. This class consisted of students who were Black, White, Hispanic, and other racial origins. After a few days of teaching these children, I came to the conclusion that they were not problematic; they only needed someone to help them to believe they were special and could succeed. I developed the philosophy that all children can learn and that there is no such thing as bad children; they only needed adults to help reverse their bad circumstances.

With this philosophy of education, my classroom became what my principal called "a model classroom." He often referred to my class when encouraging other teachers to believe that their students could have the same kind of success. I was convinced that with high expectations, great things could transpire in the classroom. I never used my students' past failures negatively, but I used positive strategies during my daily instruction.

My philosophy of discipline was seasoned with love. I often referred to it as the "Discipline with Love" approach.

I was a serious, firm, and fair teacher. I believed that a positive classroom atmosphere promoted unlimited hope for the success of all students. I will never forget how my principal encouraged me in a faculty meeting, referring to me as a gifted teacher who related well to all of his students and coworkers.

The teachers at Lincoln School developed an unusual, family-like rapport with each other. We were an exceptionally cordial and friendly staff, but we referred to each other with the titles of Mr., Ms., and Mrs. We also dressed and conducted ourselves professionally at all times. We were all very helpful and kind. The atmosphere of our school set a tone that enhanced the success of our efforts to make a positive difference in the lives of all of our students.

In retrospect, I perceive my transition from Jackson to Davenport as one of the greatest and courageous endeavors of my life. Like Abraham, I journeyed to a land I knew not, with my Bible in one hand and my suitcase in the other. I had a strong conviction that great things were about to happen in my life.

I developed close relationships with the staff. Among the men with whom I was close were Winston Mikel, a native of Mississippi and sixth-grade teacher; Willie Owens, the gym teacher; and Ellis Collins, the art teacher. We were like brothers.

Among the women with whom I was close were Artina Holmes-Webb and Ethel Coleman. I will always be thankful for how God placed Artina and Ethel in my life. Both of them are honorary members of the Gospel Mission Temple Church family.

Artina was a school counselor and native of Mississippi. She became like a sister to me and was there for me in every way. She even gave me motherly advice. To this day, Artina and I are very close. Artina accompanied me when I purchased my first car in March 1973. It was a 1973 gold Buick Century. At her wedding, I was honored with the role of giving her away to the groom. Those were some awesome days.

Ethel Coleman was the reading specialist. She still holds a very special place in my life and in the hearts of my whole family. Ethel and her husband, Reed Coleman, along with their children, are like an extended family to us. My wife and I consider her as our dear sister, indeed. Ethel has always been there during our celebrations, triumphs, and adversities. She and her family are a very important part of my family.

In 1973, my brother Eddie came to live with me. He enrolled at Palmer Junior College and graduated two years later. He then enrolled at St. Ambrose College, graduated, and became a teacher in the Davenport Community School District.

All of my brothers and sisters have played key roles in loving and supporting me along my courageous journey of life. I will always be grateful to them, their spouses, and their children. I must give some very high honor to my sister Evangelist Annie Pickett. She is one of God's most illustrious and anointed vessels. Evangelist Pickett has nurtured and invested in me all my life. God used her to help me through my successful high school and college years, and she tremendously promoted my ministry. Our church family has been blessed by her great, godly wisdom and counsel down through the years.

May all of my siblings and their future generations be blessed with God's richest favor. May their names go down in the archives of divine history. To them, I bestow my summa cum laude, my highest honor.

6

Chosen to Answer the Call

Make your calling and election sure.
2 Peter 1:10

After teaching in the Davenport Community School District for several years, I met my wife, Michelle. I shall never forget the first time I saw her. I was dining at Bishop's Buffet in downtown Davenport. She was dressed like a queen in her Sunday-go-to-meeting suit. It was love at first sight. I inquired about her and asked which church she attended. I visited her church and introduced myself to her mother, grandmother, and pastor. I offered my services to play the organ for the choir in which she sang, and the rest is history. We were married on June 6, 1981, which was one of the happiest days of my life.

In 1981, shortly after my marriage, I was deeply overwhelmed by my God-given call to the ministry.

Two years later, on November 20, 1983, I preached my first sermon at Christ Temple Cathedral Church in Chicago. Later that year, I began teaching Bible study at my apartment, with my brothers Eddie and Roy. After teaching Bible study for a few months, our mission church, Gospel Mission, was born. Our first official services were held in the basement of our home. My first congregation consisted of my wife and children, my brothers Eddie and Roy, and their families.

We outgrew the basement of our home and rented the Friendly House, located at 303 Taylor Street. After worshipping there for about three years, we purchased our first church edifice at 2202 West Fourth Street for seventy-five thousand dollars. One of my fathers in the ministry, Bishop Obadiah McInnis, was the dedicatory speaker. It was at this location that we experienced tremendous favor and spiritual growth.

Gospel Mission was officially renamed Gospel Mission Temple. The church began to attract people of diverse races and social and economic backgrounds. The following article appeared in the *Quad City Times* on November 19, 1989, announcing the dedication service of the first church building located at 2202 West Fourth Street:

LIVE THE UNLIMITED LIFE

Church Finds A New Home

Members of a five-year-old Davenport congregation are giving special thanks this week for the first home of their own. They will dedicate the historic building at 2202 W. 4th St. as Gospel Mission Temple, and are inviting the public to visit the landmark sanctuary.

The dedication and open house will be at 7:30 p.m. on Friday. The bishop of their denomination, Bishop O.W. McInnis from Virginia Beach, VA, will officiate. He heads the National Churches of Christ (Holiness) USA, which was founded in 1895.

Gospel Mission Temple was founded in Davenport in 1984 by the Rev. J. R. Horton, present pastor. Meeting space was rented at Friendly House at 303 Taylor St. Now that there is a place to call home, development of several new outreach programs are under way. Rev. Horton said, "Programs such as alcohol and drug abuse counseling, job rehabilitation and recruitment, a caring concern for senior citizens project, and a food pantry is top of the list."

> The church on Fourth Street was built in 1902 as Berea Congregational Church with a nucleus of West German Immigrants. In 1983, it was inducted into the National Register of Historic Place. Outstanding elements of its unusual architecture are the stained glass windows. Some of their designs are particularly suitable for the Thanksgiving dedication. One with a sheaf of grain represents the harvesting of souls. The inscription in German is "The harvest is plentiful." Another reads "If you love me, keep my commandments."
>
> Angie Bone, a native of Germany who lives in Davenport, visited the church to translate the inscriptions. The artist has not been identified, but the church is researching the work. "We've been told it's the highest quality of glass," Rev. Horton said. The new congregation moved into the church about a month ago. It had been used for several years by the Bible Missionary Church.

Because of this enormous growth, I was compelled to retire from the school system and become a full-time pastor in May 1997, after teaching for twenty-five successful years. It was at this point I organized a building construction committee.

In 1999, after much prayer, we purchased thirty-five prime acres of land at 5074 North Pine Street in north Davenport and began our building process. Our spacious building edifice was completed in December 2000 at the cost of three million dollars. The official dedication and grand opening was July 26, 2001. The event drew an overwhelmingly massive crowd from the Quad Cities and many other cities across the country. This gathering included an enormous representation of clergy, community leaders, educators, and all of my family from Jackson, Mississippi; Chicago, Illinois; and other locations. My father and mother were the most honored in attendance. The dedicatory sermon was given by the Honorable Dr. Marcus Butler of Jackson, Mississippi.

The media covered our story with a massive, front-page article that appeared in the *Quad City Times* on July 26, 2001:

> *No wonder Elder Jimmie R. Horton is singing God's praises. The family Bible study he began 17 years ago in his basement has evolved into a church that worships in a $3 million facility in Northwest Davenport—built to expand along with its growing congregation.*
>
> *Gospel Mission Temple celebrates its grand opening and dedication service at 7 p.m. Friday,*

and the public is invited to see how God blesses the faithful. Blessed is exactly what the Black, White, Hispanic, Asian, and other worshippers in a diverse congregation feel at Gospel Mission Temple. Standing inside the massive church building whose walls seem to reach to heaven, the people sing, clap, and shout their praise to God, guided by an energetic leader, a 75-member Mass Choir, a trio of talented singers, and an organist who commands spirited music from his instrument. Horton and two assistant ministers, his brothers Roy and Eddie, can't help but tap their toes to the music as they sit in high-backed chairs in the sanctuary.

The pastor, in a simple burgundy-colored clergyman's cassock, rises from his seat, moves to the podium, and breaks out into enthusiastic preaching. He related the details of everyday life to the Gospel, talking about needing more than his bowl of Cheerios or Total cereal in the morning, needing more than a cup of Maxwell House or Folgers coffee. Satisfying his hunger is a real and physical need but nothing is as satisfying as having Christ in his life, he tells the congregation. They enthusiastically agree.

"He had a long career as a school teacher. He

preaches with a good handle on where people's lives are and knows how to speak to them without insulting them or without seeming to run their lives. I think he makes the Gospel exciting and magnetic rather than condemning or judgmental," says Chuck Landon, the executive director of Churches United of the Quad City Area.

"Horton's zestful faith, down-to-earth appeal and appreciation for diversity are keys to his success as a pastor and to the growth of his church," Landon says. "I am impressed that he has been able to include a pretty significant racial diversity in his church," adds Landon, who will participate in Friday's celebration and present a Churches United Membership Plaque to Gospel Mission.

"I think one of the main reasons God allowed this church to be born was to break barriers—socially, racially, economically, and spiritually," Horton says.

The Beginning

His father and grandfather were pastors, but Horton wanted to be a teacher long before he felt called to become a pastor. The Bible study he began in his basement 17 years ago grew as family members invited friends, who invited more friends until there were about 100 people attending. Horton didn't want to inconvenience his neighbors, some of whom were coming to the Bible study, too, so the group moved into the Friendly House and started a church. From there, they moved to a church building at 2202 W. 4th St. Davenport, where they stayed until they outgrew that facility. He continued to teach while serving as pastor part-time.

Carolyn Graham, a teacher at Lincoln Fundamental School in Davenport, where Horton worked, remembers her friend and co-worker being a teacher with high expectations for his students, dealing with them in a positive and fair way. She always sensed that the ministry had a strong pull on Horton. It was very obvious that he was a very nice person.

In 1997, he knew the time had come to retire from teaching and become a full-time pastor. He says, "I was very confident because I knew that my responsibilities were so demanding in both areas. And that chapter of my life had been well done and it was time for another chapter to begin."

LIVE THE UNLIMITED LIFE

Holistic Ministry

Gospel Mission Temple hasn't grown by the sheer force of Horton's personality, although that is part of it, members say. His strict, moral principles and his emphasis on holistic ministry—meeting the spiritual, physical, intellectual, and emotional needs of people—are the church's girders.

It is a full gospel church, which emphasized a five-fold ministry: the Bible teaching of the apostles, evangelism, the ministry of teaching, the ministry of pastoring and the prophetic ministry. The church also offers 30 ministries—ranging from healing, health, and hospitality to youth outreach, senior care, and helping people deal with substance abuse issues.

"Pastor Horton follows God's lead and honors God with his very life, which makes him a good example for our church family. His love for God and God's people is very genuine and real. That's the reason the church is growing so fast. It's because people want the truth preached and to experience God's love in a real way and that is why I stay," says Norma Webb-Green, a 12-year member of the church.

Marva Teague says she felt welcomed with open arms on her first visit to the church, "I was in a very bad abusive relationship during that time, and after several visits, I asked Pastor Horton for counseling. He helped me to gain my strength, faith, and self-esteem back through the Holy Word of God," she adds

Kevin Ellis, another longtime member, arrived at the church in the midst of a painful divorce. The pastor's love toward him and the uncompromising truth Horton preaches kept him coming back for more. He also appreciated the welcoming attitude extended to people of all races and backgrounds, he said. Today, Ellis spends many hours volunteering at the church. He assisted with the new building's design and built a solid oak cross, 13 feet high and 5 feet wide, that hangs in the sanctuary. A lighted box behind the cross illuminates it. "I wanted it to be very special," he says.

Keep the momentum

Each department is helping with the church's ministries. "Their gift of service is a critical component in keeping the church going,"

Horton says. In the midst of the blessing, he reminds the congregation about the sacrifice and obedience that comes first, which Jesus demonstrated during His time on earth. Sacrifice and obedience are the other girders of Gospel Mission Temple.

"Paying $240,000 in cash for the 35 acres on which the church stands would not have been possible without the sacrifice of all of us. There are 700 members in all, with about 450 of them attending regularly, Horton says. On top of that, they have paid off $1 million of the $3 million church building's cost. "We did not have to go to any outside sources. These have come from faithful parishioners," Horton says.

Their generosity means that the church will be able to proceed with building an activity center onto the rear of the building. More building is planned—a balcony and additional pews, finishing off the education center—as growth and funding permit. "The church also intends to open a fully accredited Christian Academy at some point," Horton says. "The congregation has such a liberal spirit toward giving that all of our needs are bountifully met," he adds.

In my long history of living in Davenport, this was the first time that this level of newspaper coverage had ever been given to a church. Gospel Mission Temple has continued to prosper miraculously in God's favor. Shortly after building the massive sanctuary, we completed a second phase, which was a spacious Family Life Education Center. This promoted the founding of the Gospel Mission Temple School of Ministries, which includes over sixty ministries at present. The ministries were named in the honor of Bishop O. W. McInnis and his lovely wife, Mother Julia McInnis, whom we fondly called Dear.

Gospel Mission Temple School of Ministries

Addiction Prevention Ministry
Alter and Discipleship Ministry
Audio/Visual Media Ministry
Baptism Ministry
Bereavement Care Ministry
Brotherhood Ministry
Building Fund and Land Development Ministry
Calendar of Events Ministry
Campus Beautification Ministry
Children and Youth Church Ministry
Convalescent Care Ministry
Culinary Service Ministry
Domestic Assistance Ministry
Drama and Fine Arts Ministry
Early Childhood Education Ministry
Educational Tutoring Ministry
Financial Management Ministry
Food Pantry Ministry
Foster Care Ministry
Full Gospel Stewardship Ministry

Global Outreach Ministry
Gospel Mission Temple
 Ministerial Institute
Gospel Mission Temple
 Orchestra Ministry
Gospel Press and Publishing
 Ministry
Healing for the Hurting
 Ministry
Health and Fitness Ministry
Holistic Counseling Ministry
Holistically Free Ministry
Hospitality, Greeting, and
 Usher Ministry
Human Resources Ministry
Information Technology
 Ministry
Inspirational Music Ministry
Intercessory Prayer Ministry
Leadership, Growth, and
 Development Ministry
Marriage and Family
 Counseling Ministry
Ministers' and Deacons' Wives
 Ministry
Outreach News Ministry
Outreach Tract Ministry
Parental Support Ministry
Pastoral Assistance Ministry

Pastoral Care Ministry
Prison Rehabilitation Ministry
Provisions for Community
 Needs Ministry
Public Relations Ministry
Senior Care Ministry
Soul-Saving Assessment
 Ministry
Soul Winners Ministry
Special Community Events
 Ministry
Sunday School Ministry
Temple Prayer Ministry
The Christian Academy
 Ministry
Upper Room Ministry
Visitor Correspondence
 Ministry
Wellness Support Ministry
Witnessing Within Walls
 Ministry
Witnessing Without Walls
 Ministry
Women of Virtue Ministry
Young Godly Women's Ministry
Young Men of Valor Ministry
Youth Activities Ministry
Youth Mentoring Ministry
Youth Outreach Ministry

The value of our land has enormously appreciated, and the total of our edifice and land is appraised at over ten million dollars.

I believe God always finds vessels that are ready, eager, and longing to be used to make believers of others in the miraculous power of God. As I look back over my life, I can see that God had a predestined plan all the time for my ministry. I strongly believe that Jesus died to make it possible that whosoever will can succeed and receive the best that life has to offer. God, even to this day, is using the faithful flock at Gospel Mission Temple to be the light of the Quad Cities and to all the masses that have come.

God still speaks. I hear His inaudible voice each day reminding me of the great rewards of following and obeying Him. The blessings He has bestowed upon us are so appealing that it has made believers out of innumerable people.

I shall never forget one of the most overwhelming spiritual experiences I have ever had. It was June 11, 2005, just at the break of day, when the voice of the almighty God Himself not only spoke into my ear but into my total being, as I lay in bed in our newly constructed home.

This loving, powerful, and gentle voice said to me, *"You have never loved anybody or anything more than you have loved Me."* And after a gentle and serene pause, the voice of God continued by saying with strong emphasis, *"And I know that!"*

The joy that flooded my soul was unexplainable. A tranquillizing joy overwhelmed my total being. I wanted to arise from my bed and leap, but for that time period, it seemed I was unable to move. I will never be the same as a result of this experience.

I love God infinitely. The love I have for Him is uniquely reflected through the way I love all men, women, boys, and girls. This experience was a reassurance that God still speaks to mankind, as He did to the prophets of old. It humbles me and causes me to love and commit myself the more to the Lord. It was also another confirmation that "Jesus Christ is the same yesterday, today, and forever more" (Hebrews 13:8). I will always enjoy sharing this experience. God has not diminished in His power and ability to allow those of this age to believe and experience His ever-present power.

7

The Highest Quality of Life

It is in him you live, move, and have your being.
Acts 17:28

The quality of life is determined by its ultimate source. Have you defined your ultimate source? Since all life begins with God, our focus must be on Him. He loved us so much that He gave us the essence of Himself through Jesus. He desires that you experience life at its highest level of fulfillment. It is in Him that we live, move, and have our being.

Contrary to Darwin's theory of evolution, we did not evolve. We were created. We are descendants of God, who is a supernatural spirit. God made us in His image. He breathed into our nostrils the breath of life, and we became living souls. Our lives consist of the spiritual breath of God that indwells our human being. We are composed of a greater existence than mere human bodies. First, we are spirit, and then we are body. We are the temples of God. We are not self-existent, and we do not own ourselves. We are God's workmanship, and we are fearfully and wonderfully made (Psalm 139:14). Therefore, we should glorify Him in our body, mind, and spirit.

God did not create us to be self-sufficient. We were created to be beneficiaries of His all-sufficiency. We were not created to do only what we want to do but to live life at its best through obedience to God. Life for us is at its best when we accept the total will of God and become totally submitted to Him. Even our human joys and pleasures are intensified when we include Him in our daily lives.

Each step we take toward living our lives to its fullest potential is another step to ultimately glorifying God. God reflects His spiritual self to all humans on earth through the lives of us that represent Him on the earth. Therefore, He has made it possible that each of us may live the kind of lifestyle that will impress others to believe. For Jesus said from the Mount of Olive, "Let your light so shine before men that they may see your good works and glorify your Father which is in heaven" (Matthew 5:16).

We, even at our best, are limited human beings, and we need God's help at all times. We need supernatural help regardless of how astute, brilliant, or sufficient we may think ourselves to be. He has offered us His best by giving us hope to do whatever is necessary to succeed in life. He has given hope to all who are hopeless. His hope is all-sufficient, absolute, almighty, and unlimited. Our trust and obedience to His Word makes us recipients to the endless benefits of the best of life and living.

The more we know about Him, the more we will know about real life. Each day we should move beyond the level of knowing about Him to personally knowing Him. Each day should be another experience of enjoying the very presence of God. We need His strength to live from day to day. The psalmist David said, "The Lord is my light and my salvation. The Lord is the strength of my life" (Psalm 27:1).

As we experience a growing relationship with God our creator, we become more confident of our own God-given image. We develop an optimistic perception of life when we believe as the Apostle Paul believed when he said, "I can do all things through Christ that strengthens me" (Philippians 4:13). This is not an arrogant attitude but a confession of divine confidence and faith. This kind of attitude must not be confused with the proud, egotistical attitude of a haughty spirit. We must keep in mind that we are God's offspring, and He is our ultimate source of existence. He is the vine, and we are the branches. Because of our connection with Him, we bear God-like fruit.

How much of the abundant life do you want? The

abundant life is holistic in nature. There is no book ever written but one that contains the divine plan of God. That book is the Bible, the great book of life, and the Holy Word of God. There is miraculous power in the words of this book because Jesus said, "I come in the volume of the fulfillment of the whole book" (Hebrews 10:7). He also said, "In the beginning was the Word and the Word was with God and the Word was God. The same was in the beginning with God" (1 John 1:1, 2). This Word is the Son of God Himself.

The Word of God is more than the letters of print called Scripture. Jesus is the Living Word. If we believe it and obey, we can become recipients of its innumerable benefits. Jesus said, "If you believe on me as the Scripture has said, out of your belly shall flow rivers of living water" (John 7:38). This living water is the Spirit of the Living God. As we become daily partakers of the Word of God, we will never hunger for the bread of idleness or emptiness.

Daily mediating and partaking of God's Word is like food from heaven that makes an incredible difference in the quality of our lives. This quality of life is complete and totally fulfilling. This is what David meant when he said, "The Lord is my shepherd and I shall not lack anything" (Psalm 23:1).

One day as I was flipping channels to look for

something wholesome to watch on TV, I paused briefly when I heard a little boy say, "I see dead people, and they don't know they are dead." I thought to myself how ironic and true these words were from this movie on television. We would all be like dead men walking if we did not have the natural and spiritual breath of God. We would not be living; we would merely exist.

Our lives do not consist of the abundance of the things that we possess. Too often, individuals have been misled to seek the tangible American dream of materialism. We should first seek the things of God, and the natural things should be secondary. Life's most valuable substances are incomparably greater than the possession of the abundance of natural things.

Our purpose in life is greater than the external. What would it profit us to gain all the prosperity of natural things and lose out on our rich spiritual destiny? (Matthew 16:26). It is God's will that we prosper, both naturally and spiritually. He has promised to supply all of our needs according to His riches in glory (Philippians 4:19). "If we delight ourselves in Him, He will give us the desires of our heart and if we ask anything in His name, He will do it" (John 14:14; Proverbs 3:5).

Our lives are greatly influenced by what we allow to affect our minds and spirits. If we abide in the blessed promises of God's Word, we benefit greatly. We should encourage ourselves and others as to how our faithfulness to God gives us favor with Him. We can live daily with the encouragement that everything will work together for our good, even in situations and circumstances that may seem adverse to our well-being. God's Word is our source of life. As we believe His Word, we will experience healing of our bodies, minds, and spirits.

When Jesus fasted and prayed forty days and forty nights in the wilderness, He was tempted several times by Satan. Jesus was very hungry, and Satan tempted Him by saying, "If you are the Son of God, transform these stones to bread" (Matthew 4:3). Jesus then used the Word of God to defeat Satan. He rose with victory by exalting the truth of how we do not live by natural bread alone, but we live by the spiritual Word that comes from the mouth of God Himself. God's supernatural bread is nutritious in every aspect of our lives.

The total benefit of experiencing abundant life is determined by our relationship with God and His Word. Reading and hearing the Word is important, but we must not merely be readers and hearers; we must be doers. Jesus is the excellent example of obedience to the Word of God. He expects us to follow His example. He even encouraged His own disciples to pursue the same path that He was setting before them. God expects us to be living epistles that are visibly seen by men, women, boys, and girls. Through the application of the full gospel, we can live life to its absolute fulfillment.

With this in mind, we must remember that when God, through His Word, gives us so much abundance, we should graciously give back to others, that they may also be partakers of these blessings. He graciously gives to us and expects us to multiply though our service by serving others. All of the gifts we receive from God should compel us to express Christ-like servitude within us. We are debtors, both to the Greeks and the Barbarians, the polished and the unpolished, and the affluent and the poor.

Our commitment to the total submission to His Word enhances our powerful relationship with the almighty God. Sometimes even the most well-meaning church members are not aware of the truth that religion without a relationship with God is dead. We must also remember that faith without godly works is dead. It is very important that we become familiar with the reality of who God is and who He wants us to be. We must be subject to living the holy lifestyle that He expects us to live.

God wants us to be as He is. He has already reminded us in His Word that He wants us be holy as He is holy (1 Peter 1:16). He expects us to conduct our lives in such a manner that we reflect to others the nature of His holiness.

It is of the utmost importance that every individual attend a church where the full gospel is absolute and sure. The impartation of the Word in any congregation should compel every pastor and preacher to preach the uncompromising truth. When a shepherd loves his congregation, he gives them a *full plate*. He does not cheat the congregation by saying only what he thinks the people want to hear. He preaches what the people need to hear, according to the Word of God.

It is good to read your Bible in the privacy of your home, but the Word of God admonishes us to "Never forsake the assembling of ourselves together" (Hebrews 10:25). The question is also asked, "How can they hear without a preacher, and how can he preach except he be sent by God?" (Romans 10:14). He who teaches and preaches the truth should expect others to see him as a living example of the truth. The preachers walk should match his talk, and his talk should line up with the fullness of the Word of truth. God's Word is a lamp to our feet and a light to our path, which guides us successfully and prosperously throughout our whole lives (Psalm 119:105).

There are great benefits in hearing the Word, believing the Word, and being daily guided by it. The Word of God is spiritual. Jesus said, "If we abide in Him and let His words abide in us, we can ask anything we desire, and He will give it unto us" (John 15:7). We must remember that it is not how much Bible we know; it is how much Bible we live. If we know the truth, we should live the truth. The truth we do not know, we should live to attain.

When we live with divine guidance, we increase the volume of the quality of our lives. When we totally submit ourselves in the spirit of humility to God, we experience the progression of God's endless favor. God is unlimited in all of His goodness and His greatness. For great is the Lord, and He is great enough to be given the highest praise. "There is no end to His greatness" (Psalm 145:3). Therefore, when we trust in God, we believe He can do everything He says He can do by His almighty and endless power. His power is inestimable.

Life is not always easy. Life, even at its best, has unexpected trials, tribulations, and even sometimes disappointments. However, we can be assured that for every believer, God makes all things work together for our good (Romans 8:28). God has a way to turn all bad circumstances and situations into good ones. He specializes in transforming our darkness into light and our wrong into right. The more we trust and obey the truth of the full gospel, the more we remove ourselves from the limitations of living prosperously.

As a child, I heard the old proverb "God helps those

who help themselves." Although God does the work, we have a part to play. We have the power to remove the issues of doubt and unbelief. We can substitute our doubts and unbelief with the marvelous faith in His Word. All things are possible to those of us that believe in Him. When we believe all of God's Word, we can receive all the benefits and experience endless possibilities.

8

Born to Be Significant

Before I formed you in the belly I knew you.
Jeremiah 1:5

Oftentimes, people unwisely judge themselves and others. We should never measure our self-worth by our education, money, or social status. Rather, we should perceive ourselves through the eyes of God's Word. Every individual is a unique gift from God. The good news of the gospel makes it clear that God is the God of no respect of persons. For God so loved the world that He gave His one and only begotten Son that whosoever believes in Him should not perish, but have everlasting life (John 3:16). The *whosoever* of the gospel makes every person that is born into this world significantly significant. Even little children are very sensitive to the unfairness of respect of persons. They know when they are discriminated against.

As a classroom teacher, I learned many great truths about the importance of treating everyone uniquely special. I learned from observation and interacting with children of diverse social, economic, and racial backgrounds that all of them wanted to love and to be loved. Much of my success as a teacher can be attributed to my God-given passion to love everybody. This love was very apparent to all of my students. I was able to discipline children with chronic problems because I disciplined with a love that was very apparent to each of them. Life is about love and being loved. When these children were convinced I cared about them, they were tremendously motivated to respect me. This enhanced their potential to learn.

As a teacher of twenty-five years, I never sent one child to the office to be disciplined by the principal, but many times I assisted the principal in counseling students who had discipline problems. These young people were easy to correct when they sensed that the correction was accompanied by love for them and for their well-being. This kind of love is also demonstrated through relationships that I have with members of my congregation and certainly with all my family at home. People don't care how much you know until they know how much you care.

One of my most favorite matriarchs of the Bible is

Mary, the mother of Jesus. God's choice of Mary is a perfect example of how He chooses ordinary people to do super extraordinary things. She was not a socialite or considered a celebrity. She referred to herself as a handmaiden of the Lord and a woman of low estate. We are all God's choice, and that is what makes all the difference.

Regardless of who may want to look down on you, you are significant. Be assured that you are fearfully and wonderfully made for a divine purpose. When mankind realizes the value of every human, the world will be a better place to live. Human prejudices have no legitimate basis upon which to substantially stand. There is no logic that can support any form of human bigotry. It is absolutely ridiculous to demean anyone who is a part of our interrelated humanity.

God has a purpose for every human being. Jesus died to save even the person who considers himself the worst of sinners. God loves sinners. He loves sinners so much that He died to make them recipients of His redemption power. It was by the blood of Jesus that God showed His love the most toward sinners. He died for us all and gave us life that we may become heirs of God and joint heirs with Christ Jesus.

Although God hates sin, He loves the sinner with great passion. He came to transform sinners to saints. "While we were yet sinners, Christ died for us" (Romans 5:8). "'All souls are mine,' said the Lord" (Ezekiel 18:4). He did not come to call the righteous but the sinners to repentance. Therefore, all mankind is significant, regardless of past or present circumstances. It is of great importance that parents, teachers, ministers, community leaders, and all adults remain mindful of how their influences affect our youth.

Recently, I attended the visitation services of the father of one of my former students, whom I taught about thirty-seven years ago. It was amazing how his daughter, Autumn, remembered my love of creative writing and literature and the teaching of proper grammar. Most of all, she remembered how I cared for all students. Autumn's parents were very fond of me. Her father was a Caucasian attorney who had successfully fought for the cause of civil rights for many minorities. She vividly recalled how courageously I dealt with the racism that existed at the school. She expressed how I had influenced her choice of becoming a professional writer and poet. It is not uncommon for children to be influenced by those they admire, regardless of their race.

As a classroom teacher, I never referred to any of the children's cumulative records that stigmatized their academic or social past. I gave them a new beginning and a new start. Because of their unfair stigmas, many students were performing at levels of unfair expectations. Children usually give what is expected of them. If children are encouraged to believe they can achieve, then they will succeed in their pursuit of achievement. If you tell Johnny that he is a bad boy, he will demonstrate how bad he can really be. Sometimes good people make bad choices. We must remember that at some time in our lives, we have all needed God's forgiveness.

The Word of the Lord says, "For all have sinned and come short of the Glory of God" (Romans 3:23). We were all born in sin, but thank God for Jesus. He died to save us from all of our sins. "Therefore, if any man, woman, boy, or girl be in Christ, he or she is a new creature. Old things are passed away and behold all things have become new" (2 Corinthians 5:17).

When we accept Jesus as our Savior, we are absolutely free from sin. We should never refer to ourselves as sinners saved by grace. We are born-again believers who are saved by grace. Jesus did not die to leave us as victims of sin. It is an insult to the power of His blood to refer to an individual who has been washed in His blood as a sinner. "If we confess our sins, He is faithful and just to forgive our sins and to cleanse us from all our unfaithfulness to God" (1 John 1:9). His blood and His grace are greater than all sin. It is best said through the prolific lyrics of John Newton's "Amazing Grace":

Amazing Grace, how sweet the sound,
That saved a wretch like me.
I once was lost but now I am found,
Was blind but now I see.

There is no condemnation to those of us who belong to Christ, because we no longer seek to please our fleshly passions, but we seek even more to please our inner-spirit person. After Christ saves us, He never wants us to fall back into the practice of sin, because He died to save us from all sin.

There was a woman in the Bible who was caught in adultery. Jesus completely forgave her and told her to go and sin no more. The nature of a sinner is slavery to sin, but the nature of a true Christian is the liberty of walking in the freedom of salvation. As God is righteous, He expects us to daily live lifestyles that are in tune to obedience of His Holy Word.

Holiness is not a religious denomination. Holiness is the nature of God, transformed supernaturally into the hearts of mankind. It becomes a precious and blessed lifestyle to all of its recipients. Without it, no man shall see the Lord (Hebrews 12:14). We are so blessed to have access to the empowerment of being indwelled and being led by His Spirit. Jesus was given to us as our Savior. The Holy Spirit is our keeper and supernatural power to conduct ourselves in a godly manner that pleases Him.

God had something very special in mind when He chose you to be born. God has good taste. He never would have chosen you if He did not preconceive a good plan for your life. Each of us is uniquely different. Every one of us, in unique ways, has been chosen by God to make an indelible difference in making this world a better place to live. You are God's special choice. You are God's chosen generation, royal priesthood, and holy nation. You are part of a special people, which is the family of God. You have been called out of darkness into the marvelous light to praise and magnify Him daily (1 Peter 2:9).

It is of paramount importance that every one of us considers the high price that Jesus paid to make it possible for us to excel in every area of our lives. Never measure your self-worth by external, insignificant stereotypes of society. Who you are is more significant than what you own. Materialistic blessings are a part of God's plan, but true riches are greater than the possession of things. Jesus said, "A man's life consists not in the things he possesses" (Luke 12:15).

Our society has unjustly and unwisely created a false success image that has led many to experience tragedy and pain. Yes, we should appreciate the blessings of natural possessions, but we must put these natural possessions in their proper place. It is God's will that we have and enjoy economic prosperity. The Lord said,

"Try me and see how I will open the windows of heaven and pour you out blessings that you will not have room enough to receive" (Malachi 3:10). God is a God of more than enough. Enjoy it and be blessed. We are the sons and daughters of Abraham who are extremely wealthy.

The Lord has enormously blessed my wife and me to prosper with many of these materialistic things. We have these things, but these things do not have us. The more we receive, the more we give. God never intended that we only have enough for ourselves.

While walking the streets of a certain neighborhood in Jackson, Mississippi, I discovered there were individuals who were good people in spite of their unfortunate circumstances. As I walked, I befriended some of them. I shared with them my testimony and the goodness of the Lord. It was obvious that they were inspired by my friendship. It is not to be assumed that all people of low estate are not open to those who want to love and help them. Jesus was compelled to go through a town called Samaria because the people of Samaria were rejects.

With this same compassion, I took my walk through this neighborhood among a people whom I considered diamonds in the rough. I could hear an inaudible voice say, *"These are my people; I have no respect of person."* It was with joy that I responded and said to myself, as Jesus did, "I, too, must go through Samaria."

When Jesus met a certain woman of Samaria at the well, He treated her as we all should treat those who are less fortunate. He gave this woman a new self-image by offering her a spiritual well of salvation and living water.

We should never judge ourselves or others by the measuring tools that may, in any way, demean us. Too often, individuals underestimate their own self-worth. Oftentimes young people unwisely fall prey to bad choices by seeking love from all the wrong places. This often ends in heartbreak and disappointment.

Our significance is of God and not of man. We should not marry or date another person seeking to improve our self-image. One must feel significant as a single person before he or she can feel significant as a married person. Be sure you do something every day to feel better about yourself. Look into the mirror and remind yourself that you are a special creation of God who uniquely possesses endless possibilities. Never expect others to treat you better than you treat yourself. You will find that most people will give you the respect they perceive you have for yourself.

You are not an accident or a coincidence. When you were conceived, a biological miracle took place. The laws of biology yielded to the will of God's choice to choose you over millions of other probabilities.

According to the factual explanation in the *Johns*

Hopkins Family Health Book, your human life began with the union of a prepared egg from your mother and with the single sperm from your father, which depended on the orchestration of interrelated mechanical, hormonal, and chemical forces. You are the result of a single fertilized egg, which was chosen from among millions. The fertilization of the egg occurred because it encountered viable sperm within a few days after ovulation. Your father propelled millions of sperm, which swam on their own power into the fallopian tube, where they encountered the waiting egg. One sperm broke through the egg's protected shell and penetrated it. Many sperm cells tried to break through, but only one succeeded in reaching this ultimate goal.

In spite of all the many possible variables and difficulties that could have risen along the way, about nine months later you were born. This alone proves that you are greatly and uniquely significant and that God had a unique plan for you before you were born. Your self-worth and purpose is immeasurable. The plan of God for your life on earth is of great and everlasting importance. No circumstances or adversity should ever intimidate your self-image.

Habitually encourage yourself. This is very necessary in developing wholesome self-worth. William Shakespeare wrote in *Hamlet*, "To thine own self be true." When we are true to ourselves, then we will not be false to others. Every good gift comes from God, but every one of those gifts have "divine strings attached." Remember, with everything that God gives us, He expects it to multiply to the advantage of others. A good self-image is of paramount importance. What we think of ourselves can positively or negatively affect others, because our attitude toward ourselves can provoke similar attitudes in others.

The development of good people-skills is of great importance. Our success in life can be much determined by how we relate to our family, friends, and others. Getting along well with people is also of great importance in the workplace. Getting along with others does not mean compromising our conviction or personal values. We can be positive and cordial without condoning unethical behavior. Treating people respectfully, many times, will convert difficult people into lovable individuals.

A good life is a life of constant giving of one's self and resources. The successful life can be calculated by the sum total of servitude consistently throughout life. People who give are wealthy people. Those who possess attributes of liberal service shall multiply in their own personal life. It is in giving that we always receive. The giver is greater than the receiver. "Give and it shall be given unto you pressed down, shaken, and running over" (Luke 6:38).

The head of the house must be the greatest in

responsibility and service. God expects more from the head of our home, our nation, and other institutions in society. He who would be the chief should be the servant. Husbands, indeed, must be servants to their wives and their families. Women should have high expectations for their husbands and think very highly of themselves. The reflection of a woman's own self-worth can be perceived by the choice of the man she chooses to date and marry. We should be sure to make choices in all of our relationships that will yield the positive outcome of blessings, not disappointment and torment.

No institution on earth is greater than the union of a man and woman, uniting in holy matrimony, symbolizing the divine union and relationship of Christ with His church. Marriage is the foundation to the natural and spiritual church. The family is the catalyst and pillar of our society and world. Good husbands make good fathers and good heads of households.

God's Word admonishes husbands to love their wives as Christ loved the church for which He gave His life. The husband's love for the wife should compel him to be a great provider, protector, and unselfish servant. My son Jimmie Jr. encouraged me with a written composition that he wrote several years ago as a tribute to me, when I was honored as a former educator in the Davenport Community School District:

LIVE THE UNLIMITED LIFE

My Father
Bishop Dr. Jimmie R. Horton Sr.
He is many things to me—a spiritual leader,
a teacher, and a great father.
He is an advocate of faith and moral conduct.
As a great teacher, he has affected the eternity of many.
His spiritual influence is perpetual.
As a father, amidst his many roles,
he has never neglected his role in our home.
From him I have gained an understanding
of what is most important in life.
He has taught me the value of public
servitude by his active role in society.
The life lessons and values that he taught me are reflected
as a good example of Christ's great commandment.
"Thou shall love the Lord thy God with all thine heart, soul,
mind, and strength-and love thy neighbor as thyself."
These words are directing the purpose and fulfillment of my life.
Bishop Jimmie R. Horton has taught me many things as
my spiritual leader, my schoolteacher, and my father.
His impact on my life and many others is immeasurable.
With love and honor from your son,
Jimmie R. Horton Jr., MD

The most outstanding comment from this tribute was when he referred to me as being a very busy man with enormous responsibilities in society but never neglecting to be a good husband and good father at home.

My son Avery has often encouraged us by saying that he plans to return the tremendous love we have given to him a thousand times. Wow, how encouraging! My daughter, Faith, through her sweet and kind daily devotion to us, makes us exceptionally happy to have been blessed with a daughter of such high quality of virtue and ladylike characteristics.

On Michelle's forty-ninth birthday, we had dinner together and spent an evening in the park, feeding the squirrels. We reminded each other of how marriage and life grow sweeter as the days go by. She often tells me I look just as handsome in my sixties as I did on our wedding day. Likewise, I tell her how she has grown to be more beautiful than ever.

Our children will always have our unconditional love, and we are certain we will always have a special place in their hearts. As a little girl, Faith referred to herself as "Daddy's girl." She often testifies in church of her great appreciation and thanks to God for the blessing of parents who reared her to be a virtuous young lady. Avery once said to me that the greatest compliment he had received was when someone said to him, "You are just like your father." It is obvious that Jimmie Jr. and Hannah love us tremendously. They are very special to us in many ways.

LIVE THE UNLIMITED LIFE

Family and friends are gifts that never stop giving. They give joy, love, and enormous fulfillment in life.

The blessings of a God-fearing household are blessed by these words from Holy Scriptures: "Blessed is everyone that fears the Lord and obeys Him; for God will bless them to eat the labor of their hands. You will be happy and it will be well with you. Your wife will be as a fruitful vine by the side of the house, and your children will be like olives plants around the table" (Psalm 128:3). The revitalization and resurrection of the strong family structure in our society is very crucial in our world today. Healthy, wholesome, and holy values are mandatory in our pursuit of happiness and well-being, now and in the future years of our nation and world.

There is hope for individuals born into the typical dysfunctional environment. The prophet Isaiah compared Jesus to a root out of dry ground (Isaiah 53:2). He was not thought to be born of a noble status, according to the society of that day. The question was asked, concerning Jesus, "Can any good thing come out of Nazareth?" (John 1:46). Nazareth apparently, at the time of Jesus' birth, had a bad moral and religious reputation.

In spite of all the negatives that may have affected our beginnings, God specializes in bringing good people out of less fortunate situations. "For at one time, we were all without Christ being aliens from the commonwealth of Israel and strangers from the covenant of promise. Having no hope, we were without God in this world. But now in Christ Jesus we, who sometimes were afar off, are now made nigh by the blood of Christ" (Ephesians 2:13). This means we were once lost, but we are now saved and brought into the family of Christ through His shed blood.

The hope of each of us is interrelated to the hope that affects all of us. When we see others through the eyes of Christ, we become examples of the compassion that Christ has shown toward us. We all, in some way, have been made better by someone else. Every time we see someone who is less fortunate than we are, we should say, "If it were not but for the grace of God, there I go."

I have a special concern for all people; especially for those who are less fortunate. Many of the less fortunate are the minority citizens across our nation. In my hometown of Jackson, Mississippi, remarkable change has taken place in the structure of public office and higher-ranking leadership. The mayor, the superintendent of schools, and most city council members are African American. When I was a little child, the possibility of this level of minority leadership was almost an impossible dream. This is indeed progress, but we need to do more to promote and assure progress, not only among the minority but among our majority citizens.

Many young men and women are not embracing

values that have worthwhile benefits for their future. Many of them are very fine, young people who need structure and direction in their lives. The lifestyles that consist of destructive habits such as drugs, violence, crime, and promiscuous living seem to be dominating many of their lives. On the other hand, there are many young people who are contradicting the negative lifestyle and are making very positive choices in life. They are doing well in school and taking measures to mentor other youth in the community.

The Bible reads, "Train up a child in the way he should go, and when he is old, he will not depart from it" (Proverbs 22:6). We are standing on this promise concerning all of our children and the generations to follow. They, like all humankind, have made mistakes, but we know that by faith, the rich promises of our God will be fulfilled through all our generations. There are many other youth in our church and community who are leading the way in modeling a positive image to others. The superintendent of education and other community leaders have often made reference to the excellent example that the youth department of Gospel Mission Temple has portrayed to the community.

Parental involvement has always been one of my main emphases in education and all areas that concern our youth. Parents who are involved with their children will improve their total self-image, as well as their holistic self-worth.

God foreknew all of us, and He has a blessed and divine plan for us to be transformed and victorious in all things.

9

Hope for Marvelous Change

Behold, I will do a new thing and it shall surely spring forth.
Isaiah 43:19

In past years, African Americans could not truly say that America was "one nation, under God, indivisible, with liberty and justice for all." The American flag waved high over segregated schools, while the Mississippi state capitol elevated its Confederate flag. This was a contradiction of the liberty of justice the American flag falsely represented at that time. The Confederate flag, even to this day, is waving high over the state capitol, reminding us that America has not fully recovered from its sickening disease of the Jim Crow laws of bigotry and oppression of its racist past.

The great African American author Margaret Walker Alexander said it best in her poem, "For My People":

Let a new nation rise.
Let another world be born.
Let a people loving freedom
Come to growth.

Success is not about titles. It is about character and high ethical standards in life. We all are God's handiwork. Uniquely, each of us has great potential. We are a combination of the legacy of the patriarchs and matriarchs of our past. Our destiny is not determined only by our past and present but by the endless possibilities of our future. It is therefore unwise to judge anyone before his or her time.

God is not done with any of us yet. Our best is yet to come. David, the little shepherd boy, was the least of his father's house. Although he was the least, he was chosen from among his brothers.

Have faith in God. Have faith not just for the benefits, but have faith to provoke your good works, because faith without works is dead. God expects us to take total advantage of all the gifts, talents, and abilities that He has graciously given us, that we may make a positive difference in the world. We enhance our purpose when we help others. When we live unselfish lifestyles, we fulfill the great commission of Jesus Christ. Jesus stated this commission in Mark 16:15: "Go into all the world and demonstrate the Good News to every creature."

I am deeply concerned about our future generations. It is left up to us to encourage our youth to be motivated to seek the better way of life. We should encourage them to think constructively. It is my daily prayer that our youth stay in school and stay committed to godly standards and principles. It is also my prayer that the expectation level of our youth will escalate. Today, too many of them are irresponsible and have a false sense of entitlement, believing that society owes them something. Many of them are jobless and are not seeking employment, but there are many youth who contradict these negative statistics. God will always have a positive statistic to counteract every negative one.

There is no excuse for pessimistic attitudes in life. Regardless of how small or insignificant our resources may be, God always multiplies us when we utilize what we already have. God once asked Moses, "What is that in your hand?" And Moses replied, "This is my rod" (Exodus 7:9). God instructed him to stretch it out; upon his obedience, the rod miraculously turned into a serpent. The rod was transformed, signifying that miracles happen when we obey God in doing what we can with what we already have. When we act on God's Word, we can always see God demonstrate Himself, as only He can, in great and miraculous ways.

I remember when I was first ordained as pastor

of Gospel Mission Temple. Bishop McInnis (one of my fathers in the gospel) would often say, "There is power on your knees, but always know when it is time to arise from your knees and be used by God to answer your prayer." What we say on our knees must be activated by the action that takes place after we rise. The old folks would often remind the young people that God helps those who help themselves. God has put rods in all of our hands. I am convinced that God, through His Son, Jesus Christ, has made it possible for all of us to be victorious and successful every day in every area of our lives. God never leaves us helpless. He wants each of us to be greatly blessed by having all of our needs met. When He blesses us, it enhances our witness for Him. His blessings will shine through us, compelling others to desire His awesomeness.

A Black man leading our nation is a revolutionary change. In contrast to America's dark, racist past, a Black president in the White House is indeed an amazing American miracle. The greatest joy of his election, however, should not be merely because of his skin color but because God has blessed us with a man who qualifies to lead our nation to radical, social, and economic change in America and the world. Even so, the president cannot do it by himself. We all have a unique role to play in making that positive difference to improve our country.

Remember, what you do in your house must coordinate with our pursuit for change in the White House. Society must begin with the promotion of high morals and spiritual values in our homes. These values must be taught and demonstrated by the parents and passed on to the children of our present and future generations.

Our country has seen some improvements from the ugly stereotypes of the dark past of America, but there is much more that needs to be done. It is very obvious that a miraculous change has come. If America is to be a great nation, it must rise to the true meaning of its creed of liberty and justice for all. Our nation, as a whole, will benefit enormously when it considers every part of humanity as a necessity in fulfilling the American dream. A minority holding public office is progress for the United States of America as a whole. As Dr. Martin Luther King Jr. said, "The destiny of America is tied up with the destiny of each individual citizen of America." It is of great importance that credible individuals are elected to lead our nation. However, they can't do it by themselves. We all have a unique role to play in making the positive differences to improve our country.

The bitterness of bigotry and racial strife must end in order for America to experience the reality of its highest potential. Barack Obama's parents were interracially married and he, like many other citizens, experienced negative, stereotypical reactions from racist America. Any other form of racial prejudice is a disease that can only be cured by the power of love. The Reverend Dr. Martin Luther King Jr. said he would love to "speed up the day" when all of God's children, Black men and White men, Jews and Gentiles, Protestant and Catholic—would be able to join hands and sing in the words of the old Negro spiritual, "Free at last, free at last, thank God Almighty, we are free at last."

We should not allow any facet of society to smother us with bigotry, whether religious, social, or economical. We should not be divided by political differences, whether Democratic or Republican. We should not be divided by a liberal America or conservative America. We should consider all of us as citizens of the United States. We should not be divided by a Black America or a White America, a Latino America or an Asian America. We should be unified as a United States of America.

We may not agree with all of the president's policies or his political opinions, but we all must agree that he is a symbol of revolutionary change for the betterment of the American people.

Again, I must reiterate that bigotry in any form is an evil and cancerous disease that can only be cured by the power of God's love and forgiveness. We must also guard against the evils of biases that are associated with the clashing of social classes. Remember that with God, there is no Jew or Greek, no high social class or low social class, but *whosoever will* is the key to the unity of our nation and world.

While watching *The Little Rascals* on television, I was saddened by the stereotype of the little Black child named Buckwheat. *The Little Rascals* portrayed Black children as stupid, dumb, and lazy. This image was portrayed in some of the first shows that included Blacks on television. The American film industry has made some progress, but it still has a long way to go. The Black history curriculum in our school system is not giving due credence to the total Black history of America. I am convinced that when we change the mentality of the biased attitudes of society, we will hasten social progress, which is still much needed in our cities across the nation and the world. One cannot hold down another without hindering his own mobility.

Protect your self-image. Be not enslaved by a negative self-perception. When counseling our youth, I encourage them to remain free from negative peer pressure. I often say how important it is to always do the right thing at all times. It is important they know it is not cool to be a fool.

There are many fads that jeopardize the lives of the youth of our society. Many of these fads encourage our youth to engage in lifestyles that can be destructive. These lifestyles can also affect other people. Our society should ban vulgar music that disrespects and demeans women.

Much of the music industry is filled with contamination-breeding, ill-mannered youth. It is important that they dress to reflect positive role modeling. Certain employers will not accept a male applicant for an executive position if he shows up for the interview with sagging pants, body piercings, tattoos, and earrings. We should never underestimate our message to others through the way we dress. Sometimes our nonverbal language speaks louder than our verbal language. A good name is better than riches, and our name is reflected through everything we do.

When I taught at Lincoln Elementary School, there was a mandatory dress code, which made a remarkable improvement in the structure of the school. This created an environment that promoted effective learning by the whole student body. The street mentality has played a major role in promoting much corruption in our homes, schools, and the community. This attitude rebels against constructive structure in the classroom, the home, and the community.

When students behave disrespectfully in the classroom, the learning process is seriously hindered. It is just as important for teachers to respect students as it is for students to respect teachers. Even when students misbehave, the teacher should not degrade or undermine the student in any way. Neither should teachers try to be buddies with their students. Children do not need buddies in their teachers or parents. They need adults to be the guiding force that they can look up to. Again, we must remember they don't care how much we know until they know how much we care.

I experienced much of the greatest success of my twenty-five years of teaching with students who were mislabeled. These young people simply needed positive reinforcement to make them feel significant and special. Our young people desire to be disciplined. Even though they may appear to rebel, many times their rebellion is seeking the attention of someone to care enough to show them love through guidance and counseling. Many times even those children who were born to be leaders will go to the extreme with negative behavior, crying out for discipline.

Unfortunately, our homes, schools, and churches have shown a great decline in the establishment of positive yet stern rules and regulations that will establish order. I often say that where there is not enough discipline, there is no order. Where there is no order, there is no structure. Where there is no structure, there is no productivity.

Proper discipline is a building tool that establishes a sure foundation in our lives. Jesus said it best when He said, "He who builds his house upon a rock is like a wise man that builds his life upon the solid Word of God and when the storms of life come, the house will stand on the sure foundation" (Matthew 7:24).

10

Live Your Life by Faith

*Faith is the substance of things hoped for
and the evidence of things not seen.*
Hebrews 11:1

When we live by faith, we live with endless possibilities. Faith establishes a strong confidence in God's Word. I attribute all of the success in my life to the foundation of my wholehearted trust in God's Word. The psalmist David said, "Trust in the Lord with all your heart and lean not to your own understanding but in all your ways, acknowledge Him and He will direct your path" (Proverbs 3:5). When we have faith in God, we believe that God is who He says He is, and He can do everything He says He can do. Faith makes us accessible to all that God has and all of who God is. All things are possible to those of us who believe. The power of faith affects our whole person. The spirit of faith and the mind of faith can affect our destiny in life. When we believe we can do great things, according to our faith, it will be done unto us. You are what you think you are. We must have the attitude that we can do all things through Christ, who is our strength. It is my goal to practice this kind of faith every day. Faith is more than our believing that we may receive; faith is a lifestyle!

The Bible patriarch Abraham has been given the title of "Our Father of Faith." God declared that all of Abraham's spiritual seed would be highly favored and blessed by the hands of the almighty God. We are Abraham's seed. We are heirs of faith. Faith also seeks to please God. Without faith, it is impossible to give God the respect He deserves. Everything we do should be done by faith, because that which is not done of faith is sin. Sin is mankind's greatest enemy.

We are not to live by chance. Life is too serious; never gamble with it! Individuals who gamble are trusting in luck and not in God. This can become an addiction that preys upon the human weakness of seeking to get something for nothing. The promises of God are sure. For He said, "I will supply all of your needs according to my riches in glory" (Philippians 4:19). The gambler is not building his hope upon certainty. Even those who may win, win only to lose again. Life is sweet when we can walk in the blessed assurance that God is absolute about everything that pertains to us. Faith brings peace of mind, which develops optimism and gives us the power to think positively. My father and mother made us accessible to all the best things in life when they taught us to trust in the almightiness of God.

There is no human being that can be everything to us like God. He is not only sufficient, but He is all-sufficient. Faith believes that, although I am limited in my human abilities, with God there are no limits. Faith transforms all of our negative confessions into positive confessions. We should stop saying "I can't" and start saying "I can." When we apply the faith concept to all of our relationships, we develop more healthy and wholesome experiences with others. A good relationship with God enables us to establish good relationships with others.

Faith helps us to accentuate the positive. I have learned that my faith in God enhances positive interactions with my family members and others. Faith helps us to believe that all of our unfortunate circumstances are temporary. God's Word is full of positive benefits. We need to believe that future generations will prosper because of the faith of their fathers and mothers before them.

We are trailblazers for the next generation and every generation thereafter. As I lay prostrate in my prayer room each morning, I nourish my faith with prayers of faith. My daily petition is, "Lord, use me and use my future generations to love You as we grow stronger in our praises toward You. Grant us the wisdom, strength, riches, glory, honor, and blessings to multiply as greater witnesses for You each day."

Every believer has faith. It was faith that caused you to believe unto salvation. You were born out of faith to believe God's plan of salvation and accept Christ as the pardoner of your sins. Just a little faith can move the mountains in your life. However, the more you trust in His Word, the more you will grow into a greater relationship with God. We have many patriarchs, both living and dead, who have demonstrated great acts of faith that can enhance our trust in the promises of God. Therefore, because we have been blessed with so many pioneers of miraculous faith, let us then be motivated to lay aside every weight and distraction and the sin that so easily hinders us, and let us run this race with patience and not vanity (Hebrews 12:1).

Radical faith produces radical change. Jesus was and still is radical in all that He does. Jesus was radical in all of His ministering while on the earth. Many believers tend to stray away from taking a radical position in their walk with the Lord for fear of being tagged as a fanatic. This attitude tends to hinder believers from receiving all the benefits of the Christian heritage and the total sum of the favor of serving God wholeheartedly. It is God's will that all of us experience the best in life. We must believe that we can be partakers of everything that God wants us to have.

Our church attorney, Paul Bibber, complimented my radical faith one day while we conversed in his office. He said, "Bishop Horton, you and your congregation have built that huge multimillion-dollar church with all of those ministries because you did not have sense enough to know that it could not be done." He and I chuckled, and he went on to say how he remembered when we began as a mission church, possessing only a podium, a microphone, and a few chairs. His statement encouraged me to continue to believe God gigantically!

Each Sunday just before I deliver the message, I lead the entire congregation in our Word confession:

This is the Holy Word of God.
It cannot fail me.
I have found in it everything that I need.
It teaches me everlasting life.
It fills my heart with joy, wondrous joy,
Because I believe in Him who is able to do exceeding,
abundantly, above all, that I am able to ask or think
According to the power and authority of the almighty God.
In Jesus' name, I am somebody.

I am who His Word says I am.
I can do everything that His Word says I can do.
I will have everything His Word says I can have.
I will be everything His Word says I can be.
I am a chosen generation, a royal priesthood, and a holy nation,
I have been called out of darkness into His marvelous light.
And this is my season of marvelous faith, prosperity, and total victory.

There are times in life when we need miracles. We need something to happen that rises above all human possibilities and may even contradict the laws of human reason. Recently, I received a call from one of my parishioners, Missionary Vanessa Summers, who asked her doctor to relay to me by phone her miraculous healing of diabetes. When she called, I could tell by the sound of her voice that something spectacular and amazing had happened. She said, "Bishop Horton, I am with my doctor, and she has something exceptionally wonderful to tell you." Her doctor then said, "Bishop Horton, continue to teach and preach faith to your congregation, because it has caused Vanessa to experience a miracle. I have medical proof that she no longer has any sign of diabetes! She has been miraculously healed!" The doctor went on to say that this miracle has caused her own faith to move to another level. I commended Vanessa's doctor for her wisdom in giving God the glory for this supernatural intervention.

We cannot expect what we don't believe. There were two blind men who came to Jesus and asked Him to pray that they receive their sight. Jesus asked, "Do you believe what you are asking?" They answered, "Yes, Lord, we believe." Jesus placed his hands on them, and they both experienced the miracle of receiving their sight immediately (Matthew 9:29). It is dangerous to seek to experience miracles without having faith in the power of God. Sometimes even Satan tries to deceive individuals to believe in his false miraculous power. We should be more fascinated with who God is than with the selfish desire of wanting Him to make life easy. He is our God, not a superficial magician.

There were men in the Bible called the sons of Sceva. These men saw the Apostle Paul do great miracles. They also witnessed him casting out evil spirits by the power of God. These men, for selfish reasons, sought to do likewise. However, these spirits, also known as demons, cried out and said, "Paul I know, and Jesus I know, but who are you?" The evil spirits came out and leaped on the sons of Sceva and prevailed against them, causing them to flee, naked and wounded (Acts 19:1-17). Perverted faith is evil. We should never use our faith selfishly to get what we want from God.

True faith seeks to please God and help others. Faith in God can take us through any circumstance, regardless of how difficult. Faith is the driving force of the Word of God. When we put our faith to work, it brings action to every promise of God. The Word of God gives hope to all of our situations. Faith is the hand that reaches out to receive the promises of God. As long as we are in our mortal bodies, we will need to fight the spirit of doubt. The Bible admonishes us to fight the good fight of faith (1 Timothy 6:12).

It is the natural work of the flesh to fear the unknown and to be full of doubt and uncertainty. However, when we put our trust in God, we can feel the blessed assurance that is reflected in the hymn "Leave It There," written by Charles Tindley:

> *If you trust and never doubt,*
> *He will surely bring you out.*
> *Take your burden to the Lord*
> *And leave it there.*

Trouble, trials, and tribulations in life are not so bad when we know what to do with them. They can be opportunities rather than pitfalls. They can allow us to put our trust in God, who will fight for us and give us total victory in all situations. Psalm 24:8 reads, "Who is this King of glory? The Lord strong and mighty, the Lord mighty in battle." God is always there for us. We can have the blessed assurance and confidence that He is able and willing to help us through every problem. He is our all-sufficient protector and provider.

When we believe God, we activate the powerful, supernatural force that moves God to act in our favor, according to His Word. God is excited and ready to act on His righteous will to benefit us. God will always do right in His own perfect way. He is our foundation of belief.

When we base our belief on His Word, it confirms the Scripture that says, "I am not ashamed or doubtful about the Word of God, for it is the power of God unto salvation and unto everyone that believes" (Romans 1:16). When we believe the truth, we can rely upon the stability of God's ability to be victorious in all things. To truly know God is to believe God. Our faith is built upon our love for Him and His love for us. His love gave us His mercy, and His mercy gave us grace. It is through our faith that we receive his grace. This is the marvelous grace that gave us salvation and redeemed us from the pit of sin by the precious blood of Jesus.

We are justified by faith, but our faith without our works is dead, and our works without our faith is dead (James 2:26). We are what we do, and we do what we believe. Even in a marriage, the couple must act on their marriage vows in order to have a real marriage. Our loyalty to God should be just as important as His loyalty to us. Faith is our spiritual covenant with God. Therefore, we should hold firmly to our commitment to God without wavering, because He is always faithful to us. He is always reliable, and He is always true. It is important that we demonstrate twenty-four hours a day, seven days a week, and 365 days a year a wholehearted devotion to Him. Faith exalts us to let our walk match our talk.

We should never abuse God's amazing grace toward us. His grace is not our permit to live a sinful life without consequences. The Scripture clearly forbids us to continue in sin that grace abound (Romans 6:1). This is something that God forbids. The grace that saved us is available to all men. It teaches us to refrain from ungodly and worldly lust and live a sober and godly lifestyle in this present world. Grace comes with a great responsibility. God expects us to come all the way out of our lifestyles of sin and turn eternally to His way of righteousness.

Jesus paid such a great price to free us from the ugliness and bondage of death. So how can we continue in sin when He has given His life to free us from the power of sin? "He who the Son has set free is free indeed" (John 8:36). The righteousness of Jesus Christ has delivered us from the curse of sin.

Our faith in God is not magic. It is the power of God in action. Faith and grace work hand in hand. Grace is the unmerited gift that delivered us from the power of Satan's curse. Faith has been the key to all of my success in life. I now see the result of my many years of teaching, preaching, and demonstrating the gospel of faith.

Faith has blessed our church to experience the supernatural power of God at work at all times. When the disciples witnessed Jesus working miracles, they were amazed. Jesus said, "These things that you have seen me do, you shall also do and even greater things shall you do in my name" (John 14:12). His disciples were able to witness the dead being raised, blinded eyes being opened, the lame walking, the deaf hearing, and the poor having the gospel preached unto them.

In our congregation, the demonstration of our faith has caused us to see the curing and complete healing of cancer, heart troubles, and diabetes, as well as all manner of other sickness and diseases. We have witnessed radical social, spiritual, and economical changes manifested through the application of our faith. When we radically believe God, we always radically see the action of His reliable Word fulfilled. "These signs will follow them that believe and in my name, they shall cast out devils, they shall speak with new tongues, they shall take up serpents and if they drink any deadly thing, it shall not harm them. They shall lay hands on the sick and they shall recover" (Mark 16:17–18).

A lifestyle lived by faith is a life of endless possibilities. When we believe God, it gives us victory to develop into our fullest potential in every way possible. We become victors and not victims in the warfare of life. "Faith speaks of those things that are not as though they were" (Romans 4:17).

I can recall many times when my household was healed of various illnesses and infirmities, which can only be credited to the supernatural healing and divine love from above. I remember how God miraculously healed my wife of what appeared to be a terminal illness during the early years of our marriage. She became gravely ill, and no medical attention helped. I anointed her with holy oil and prayed for her. Michelle miraculously experienced a full recovery. Likewise, there are many instances when my children were healed. At sixty-three years old, I can say that I have been medicine-free for over thirty years.

Medical science is a special gift from God. However, faith in God is better than medicine. Both medicine and faith coupled together work wonders. The best medicine is habitual prayer and good health habits. We should treat our bodies like they are God's special property. The Apostle Paul warned the church at Corinth about foolishly abusing their bodies, saying, "Do you know that your body is the temple of God? You are not your own" (1 Corinthians 6:19). He likewise admonished those at Rome by saying, "I beg you to present your bodies as a living sacrifice, holy, and acceptable unto God, which is our reasonable service" (Romans 12:1).

We should not abuse our bodies by sexual infidelities. When we commit these kinds of sin, it brings great hurt to the individual, the family, the church, our society, and the world. Those hurt most are the children. Many times while I was counseling students, they expressed their strong disappointment of the way in which their parents' uncommitted relationships were causing hurt and despair in their homes.

When women make poor choices in men, they make choices that can permanently scar the lives of their children and themselves. When women allow men to use them cheaply, they greatly demean themselves. This can promote generational dysfunctions. Men who use women only as the object of their desires are demeaning themselves and causing societal dysfunction. When they make poor sexual choices, they likewise cause generational cycles of trouble.

The Word of God says marriage is honorable. When a man and woman live together without marriage, there is no commitment, and without commitment, these relationships produce unhealthy outcomes. Therefore, it is imperative that we live according to laws that bring proper order to our lives.

There are endless blessings when we live as God wants us to live. We must not live lives without temperance. It is dangerous to let our natural passions foolishly control us. God can help us control our passions. When we utilize our God-given faith, we bring peace and contentment to our lives. It is God's desire to help us to be victorious in every situation and circumstance in our life, as the hymn "Yield Not to Temptation," written by Horatio R. Palmer, reads,

> *Ask the Savior to help you,*
> *Comfort, strengthen, and keep you.*
> *He is willing to aid you,*
> *He will carry you through.*

There is no temptation that we could ever face that God has not already made a way for us to overcome. As we develop confidence in God, we enhance our power to pray.

When we pray with the right motive, we experience positive outcomes. James 4:3 reads, "You have not because you ask not. You ask and receive not because you ask amiss." James was implying that when we pray with the right motive, God is always willing to answer. When we pray, we should make sure that we are not praying selfishly.

We should consider others as we make our petition to God. When we consider others, we activate our personal blessings. We should delight in being kind and helping others. This is a Christ-like spirit. Like Jesus did, we should always remember others when we pray. In His final prayer, He prayed to God for our well-being, that we be kept from the evils of this world, and that we may be one even as He and the Father are one.

The gratification of servitude to others has endless benefits. As a schoolteacher, I was greatly fulfilled to see students grow and benefit by my teaching and showing concern for them. Likewise, as the pastor of Gospel Mission Temple, it always gives me unspeakable joy when I see souls converted from the power of darkness to the power of the light in the Lord. As it is stated in the song "If I Can Help Somebody," written by Alma Bazel Androzzo:

If I can help somebody, as I pass along,
If I can cheer somebody, with a word or song,
If I can show somebody, he is travelling wrong,
Then my living shall not be in vain.

The outstanding faith story is the one about the great centurion whose servant was gravely ill. He made a special trip to find Jesus. After he found Him, he explained to Jesus that he was a man of great notoriety in society but was in need of miraculous help. He said, "Lord, my servant is at home very sick with the palsy and grievously tormented." Jesus offered to come and heal his servant, but the centurion replied, "Lord, I am not worthy that You should come to my house, but just speak the word, and my servant will be made whole." Jesus marveled at the words of the centurion and said, "I have never seen such faith in all Israel." When the centurion returned home, he found that his servant had been healed at the same hour that Christ had proclaimed his healing (Matthew 8:8–10).

Another great demonstration of radical faith is the one that tells of a certain woman who had an issue of blood for twelve years. Many physicians had taken advantage of her, and she had spent all of her money on medical bills. None of the physicians could cure her. Her condition only grew worse. When she heard that Jesus was in town, she found Him and pressed her way through the large crowd, saying, "If I could just touch the hem of His garment, I will be healed of this terrible plague." After Jesus asked who touched Him, she fell to His feet with fear. Jesus said unto her, "Daughter, your faith has made you whole" (Matthew 9:20–22). Yes, I can strongly agree with this woman of faith that just one touch from the Lord can heal all manner of our diseases, now and forever more. Therefore, let us remember, "The just shall live by faith" (Hebrews 10:38). With faith, all things are possible!

11

Faith Cometh by Hearing

Faith cometh by hearing and hearing by the Word of God.
Romans 10:17

The more Word we know and live, the more the power of faith can do its perfect work. It is becoming more and more evident to me what the Scripture means by saying, "Without faith, it is impossible to please God, for the person that seeks after God must believe that He is, and that He is a rewarder of them that diligently seek Him" (Hebrews 11:6). Our knowledge of the Word of God gives us the great advantage of obedience to the Word.

Obeying God is the key to pleasing Him in all our ways. The more we please Him, the more highly blessed and favored we are. The blessings of the Lord are greatly multiplied by our submission to God's expectations. Moses makes the plan of God very clear to us in Deuteronomy

11:13. It reads, "And it shall come to pass that if you will diligently listen to the Lord your God to observe and do all the commandments which I command you this day, the Lord will set you on high above all nations of the earth. And all these blessing will come upon you and overtake you." The Word of faith gives light to our daily walk with God.

Light, in the Scripture, is symbolic of the knowledge and understanding of the truth. When we know God's plan and understand it, we have the rich blessings of His direction for our lives. Even from the time of my childhood, I have been blessed to know the Holy Scriptures. Of all of the memories of my youth, my exposure to the Word of God at home, at church, and even at school is paramount. As in the days of Moses, God still speaks through His Word. He expects each generation to pass the legacy of the Word to the next generation.

I am strongly convinced that God is saying to this generation, "Hear, oh America, hear all ye people of the world. You shall love the Lord your God with all your heart, with all your soul, and with all your might. And these are the words that I command you this day, to diligently teach the commandments to your children and speak of them when they get up, when they go about their day, and when they lie down."

When we are enlightened by the Word, we profit daily

by the application of it. We can walk in the light of the wisdom of God's expectations and endless benefits. The Word also frees us from the terrible state of annihilations from the presence of God. By His Word, we have divine connections to His supernatural security.

God's Word sheds light on His mercy and His great favor, which allows us to be pardoned by His grace. God's mercy activates His passion to love us enormously. When we deserved death, He gave us life. When we were in the cursed state of sin, He, by His grace and mercy, gave us His endless love and the riches of His divine protection. His grace removed the guilt and sorrow of our sins and gave us His justification and unspeakable joy. The gospel of John well stated it with these words: "Behold what manner of love the father has bestowed upon us that we should be called the sons and daughters of God" (1 John 3:1). His love for us is matchless and amazing. His grace surpasses human logic and all understanding.

Without the full application of our faith, we would never receive the fullness of our divine inheritance as the children of God. Faith is our spiritual connection with the almighty God that gives us hope in all of life's circumstances. Without hope, all is in vain. Our hope is Jesus Christ, the foundation of our faith. "For it is in Him that we live, move, and have our being" (Acts 17:28). This hope gives us assurance that we can expect to be victorious, in spite of all of our adversities. This hope liberates us from the spirit of doubt and fear. Life will always present circumstances that may appear hopeless and bleak, but we can find comfort in knowing that all things are possible when we believe. There is nothing too hard for God (Jeremiah 32:27).

One of the most trying times in my life occurred on Easter in 2010 (Resurrection Sunday). I was attending our annual citywide egg hunt on our church campus, when I received a call from my brother, Pastor David, informing me that our mother had become seriously ill with what appeared to be a stroke. I began to pray for her recovery. About a half hour later, Pastor David called and reported that Mother had fully recovered. To God be the glory, she more than recovered. Her doctor was so amazed that he recommended that she discontinue all medication. He stated that she was the healthiest ninety-one-year-old person he had ever seen. She is now ninety-four years old and remains a powerful testament to the hope and powerful faith of God's miraculous healing. I am so blessed to have been taught that God is still a God of miracles. "God can do anything but fail" (Deuteronomy 31:6).

When we believe God, we can instantly experience God at work. When the worst happens, it is with this strong conviction that I believe we can rise higher than ever imagined. Our faith in God touches the inner parts of our soul and spirit and gives us supernatural abilities to receive from the storehouse of the living God. We can only reach as high as we believe.

Even the most spiritual individual must fight against the spirit of doubt. Our natural being needs the supernatural ability to rise above all of our negative circumstances and be free from the devastation that logic cognition can bring when doubt and fear dominate our minds and spirits. When we tap into our spirit being, we then overcome all things. We can trust in God's ability to take us to that realm, which promotes us to believe that we can do all things above all that we are able to ask or think (Ephesians 3:20).

Faith sustains us in our daily walk with God. It keeps us from straying from the truth. In all our daily confrontations, trials, and tribulations, we activate faith when we embrace these convictions. Jesus experienced times of destitution and stress during His time on earth. However, He never doubted God. He has been a living example of how we can trust God, even during moments of dire distress and devastation. He demonstrated to us how we can triumph, despite all negative circumstances.

One of the greatest milestones in the history of our church was the construction of our multimillion-dollar church building. It was in those first months of construction of the new building that my faith was increased to believe that God would supply all our needs according to His riches in glory. We were faced with a mega-financial obligation. Our finances were limited, and we were barely meeting our budget. After much prayer, we suddenly experienced a supernatural rise in our financial income. We then began to increase the building construction project. When we stubbornly believe God, He will manifest His amazing favor, especially when we serve Him with undaunted faith to promote His kingdom.

We experienced serious conflict with a certain building contractor who tried to take advantage of us. Even on the night of the dedication, he tried to demean us, but it all backfired on him. What he meant for evil turned out for our good. This was one of the grandest nights of my life. Our building company officials, along with the CEO and president, addressed the massive crowd with great accolades toward Gospel Mission Temple. Our attorney very eloquently addressed our triumph and victory in such a way that many stood to their feet with applause.

The contracting company that sought to do us ill went bankrupt and out of business. We did not rejoice, but we were amazed at how God always fights for His own. God, even to this day, continues to amaze us over and over again. He has prospered us and continues to do great things among us. I often say that God has made the success of Gospel Mission Temple so gigantic that all who behold it can clearly see that only He can do such a magnificent thing as this.

The greatest role models of faith are my parents. It is astounding how they have done so much with so little. This year, Mother celebrated her ninety-fourth birthday, and Dad lived to see the year of his hundredth birthday. This year they also celebrated their seventy-fifth wedding anniversary.

I can remember how Mother could cook a big pot of spaghetti, corn bread, and collard greens with only a couple of dollars. She never had access to the many conveniences that housewives have today. I recall Mom telling the story of how she used torn sheets to make diapers for her babies. She never owned a baby bed, stroller, or any of the baby "necessities." All twelve of her children were born at home. She never spent one night in the hospital after delivering a child. I will always remember how my mother could dress so fine and fashionable with the clothes she purchased at the Goodwill and second-hand store. Most of our clothes were clothes bought at resale shops. My mother was one of the best-dressed women at the church. No one ever knew where she purchased her clothing. She was and still is a very beautiful lady.

Mother is beautiful both naturally and spiritually. She always trusted in God for her needs. She always knew which home remedy to use when any of her children became ill. I so vividly remember the cod liver oil, castor oil, and lemon tea cures. Momma was a natural physician. I cannot recall any of us ever going to the doctor. The faith of our mother and father taught us survival.

Yes, we were poor in material possessions, but we were rich in the things that matter most. I remember how we learned as children to do some things for ourselves, rather than be dependent upon others. We earned our monies by doing chores for our neighbors. One of my favorite memories is the smell of Momma's molasses bread and candied yam potatoes. A bag of pinto beans, a chicken, and collard greens from the garden with cornbread were a delicious meal.

Every time I smell nutmeg, it reminds me of some of the most pleasant-tasting treats of my childhood. She always advised us to refrain from eating a lot of sweets, but we were allowed to indulge at times. Her cakes and pies during the holidays and even on weekends were most special. She baked jelly cakes, coconut cakes, chocolate cakes, pound cakes, and sweet potato pies. Her cakes were always at least three layers. She also made the best banana pudding year-round. As Jesus fed five thousand people with only two fish and five loaves, Momma fed her large host of Hortons with very little, yet somehow we always had more than enough.

12

Know Your Purpose in Life

In all thy ways acknowledge Him and He will direct thy path.
Proverbs 3:6

Life without purpose is vain. To know purpose and not pursue it is also vain. Every individual is born with a God-given purpose. God has a predestined will for each of our lives. He had a design for your life before you were born. Knowing and doing God's will for your life brings total fulfillment. You cannot know His will until you acknowledge the need for His direction. The more you know God, the more you know about your life's purpose. Your ultimate purpose is a God thing and the root of every good thing that pertains to your life. God and purpose are inseparable. It is important to know the difference in what you want for yourself and what God wants for your life.

It is amazing how the things we thought were important changes as we get older. It is important that we embrace values that are more solid and stable. As we grow older, we should grow wiser. The Apostle Paul said, "When I was a child, I spake as a child and did as a child, but when I became an adult, I put away childish things" (1 Corinthians 13:11). Unfortunately, too often this is not true with many adult individuals. Becoming older does not automatically bring wisdom. Have you heard the old proverb that says the worst fool is an old fool? Sometimes foolish lifestyles and empty values can have a domino effect that passes from generation to generation. On the other hand, wise and prosperous values can be inherited from generation to generation. Blessings and curses can be generational.

Psalm 78 refers to establishing a solid respect for God and the keeping of His Word from one generation to another. Verses 4-8 read:

> We will not hide them from their children, showing to the generation to come the praises of the Lord, His strength, and His wonderful works that He has done.
>
> For He established a testimony in Jacob, and appointed a law in Israel, which He commanded our fathers, that

they should make them known to their children.

That the generation to come might know them, even the children which should be born, who should arise and declare them to their children.

That they might set their hope in God, and not forget the works of God, but keep His commandments.

And might not be as their father a stubborn and rebellious generation, a generation that set not their heart aright, and whose spirit was not steadfast with God.

The final verse above gives hope to generational curses. Generational curses can be reversed by the power of God and wisdom. The spirit of righteousness can be visited from one generation to another. Likewise, sin can be visited from one generation to another.

Medical professionals and physicians tend to calculate medical probabilities considering family history; however, poor genetic health can be reversed. If a family member has a history of a certain disease, the following generations are more likely to follow the same pattern. Genetics can greatly affect us, both positively and negatively. In some families, longevity is very prevalent. In others, length of life expectancy is very low. However, change in behavior and health habits, as well as change in spiritual lifestyles, can strongly affect length of life and holistic health.

However, the power of God's choice is greater than the laws of genetics and nature. We can all trace some favorable and unfavorable attributes in our lineage. It is God's will that we all rise above the limitations of our natural genealogy and walk in the blessed spiritual legacy as sons and daughters of God. We were all once aliens to the common wealth of Israel, strangers to the covenant of promises, without God and without hope (Ephesians 2:12), but we are now heirs with God and joint heirs with Christ Jesus (Romans 8:17).

We are God's first choice. Even when we were ignorant of our divine inheritance, He chose us. We are a chosen generation. His choice is so powerful that it is overwhelming. The renowned concert artist Marion Anderson said, "I had no choosing in my call to music. It was my call to music that chose me." In other words, Marion Anderson was saying that God's plan for our lives is stronger than our natural will. I believe that human association brings on assimilation. Our exposure can strongly affect our destiny.

I believe I was predestined to be the preacher and

teacher to which I have committed my life. As a small child, I always loved to play church and school. When we played church, I chose to be the preacher, and when we played school, I wanted to be the teacher. I believe that my grandfather and my father greatly affected my predestined choice. Both of them were powerful preachers of the gospel, submitting to their divine call. It opened the door for me to make that same choice.

The choices we make affect our future generations. This is a serious and proven truth, an astounding fact of life. Pregnant mothers and fathers who indulge in drug-abuse lifestyles give birth to what society calls "drug babies." These babies reap the horrible consequences of the poor choices their parents made. They did not directly indulge in drugs but are affected by the generation before them. Keeping this in mind, we should take precaution as we make life choices every day. The generations of the present are also affected by these decisions. Our families, society, and world will greatly improve when we make sure to consider consequences before we act on our thoughts. All humanity has a universal and individual purpose.

Our greatest goal in life should not be full of selfish passion to fill our human and emotional cravings. Our passion should be driven by our purpose, rather than passions that will lead to undesired consequences. God has designed each of us to serve a unique and divine purpose. He does not expect us to play hide-and-seek with Him. When we, in all our ways, acknowledge Him, He absolutely will always direct our paths (Proverbs 3:6). Purpose makes life exciting and valuable.

It is God's will that each of us make sure that our heart, mind, soul, and spirit are in harmony with God. He has made provisions through His Son, Jesus, that we have full redemption from our sin. It is our privilege to be recipients of this great gift through our confession and repentance. "If we confess our sins, He is faithful and just to forgive our sins and cleanse us from all unrighteousness" (1 John 1:9). He has given us a plan for salvation that is found in Romans 10:9–10. "If you confess with your mouth the Lord Jesus, and believe in your heart that God has raised Him from the dead, then you shall be saved. For with the heart, man believes unto righteousness, and with the mouth confession is made unto salvation."

Our daily lives should reflect our conversion to the new life of salvation. Every day, we should be dedicated to live the lifestyle that reflects both Christ-like walk and talk. The purpose of God and His perfect will is reflected in His Word. When we claim to be Christians, we should reflect the Christ-like way of life. God expects us to influence others as His Son did while upon the earth.

As the pastor of Gospel Mission Temple, I have experienced the great joy of seeing God pour out His favor due to our commitment and our submission to the vision He has designed for His church. Every morning I make sure that prayer is my first priority. First, I fall to my knees by my bedside and then proceed on with special prayer in my prayer room. I rededicate, commit, and submit my total self anew to Him every morning. I am strongly convinced that the divine favor we enjoy now is the result of God's preordained choice, as well as our devout submission to His great commission. Favor always starts at the top and then proceeds down. When parents submit themselves to God, it opens the door for the children to do likewise.

As I write these lines, I am rejoicing about the good news that my secretary, Missionary Kathy Wogomon, just experienced. She was diagnosed with a form of cancer in March 2010, and on May 25, 2012, the doctor confirmed that her body was miraculously healed of cancer. She and I both attribute this miracle to the favor and submission of His will. God always hears and answers the prayers of those who have positioned themselves to receive the awesome results of petitioning the throne of God.

As Missionary Wogomon prayed for her healing, she made a covenant to God that she would give Him glory. This is my teaching to all of my parishioners. Ask

God under a covenant, and it will always come to pass. As Hannah prayed for a boy child, she promised under oath that she would give him back to God. She followed through with her promise when Samuel was born. When we choose to do it God's way, we always win.

Purpose can be promoted or hindered by those we choose to make integral parts of our lives. This is why it is of utmost importance that we make serious and wise choices in a spouse. To choose a husband or wife affects more than the individual. It affects family, society, and the world. Too often, these choices are superficially made. The choices we make today make long-lasting consequences that will affect our future. We should never choose a mate simply for external reasons, such as physical attraction or other carnal reasons. The following are the most important denominators in a relationship:

- Are we born-again Christians?
- Do we hold the same moral values?
- Are we compatible in the things that matter most?
- Are we physically attracted to each other?
- Have we discussed our goals and values for family life?
- Do we communicate well?
- How will our home be supported?
- Are we good financial planners and managers?

- Are we willing to spend our lives together, even through trials and tribulations and until death do us part?
- Are we really in love?
- Did God bring us together?

Our purpose can be strongly enhanced or hindered by the circle of family, friends, and acquaintances that have influenced decisions. It is amazing how others can influence the decisions that affect our destiny. We should never be influenced by individuals who may demean or diminish our quality of life. We should not be distracted from our wholesome goals and commitments by undesirable influences. God expects us to love everybody, but He does not expect us to have companionship with everyone who seeks our friendship. The Word of God compels us to come out from among those who may negatively influence our destiny.

It is very obvious that corruption is increasing in our society; however, we should seek to be a part of the solution, rather than stand by idly doing nothing. "We are the salt of the earth" (Matthew 5:13). We are the vessels that God desires to use to rectify the contaminated sector of our society.

I am grateful for my God-given spirit to love all people, regardless of race or social, economic, or religious backgrounds. I am not intimidated by anyone. I am often told by many that it is very obvious that I love everyone.

A relative who once lived in an area where there were many economically deprived individuals stated that he observed that each time I would visit, I would take special time to talk with all of the neighbors, regardless of who they were. They often reminded me of how God has blessed me with the humility of the Apostle Paul.

If we are to win the lost to Christ, we must treat people as He would. The Apostle Paul declared that he was a debtor to both the Greeks and Barbarians (Romans 1:14). Paul said, "To the weak, I become as weak that I may gain the weak" (1 Corinthians 9:22). He was not implying, by any means, that we should compromise our godly standard but rather that we should meet people where they are to lift them higher or win them to Christ. We should never look down on anyone who is less fortunate than we are, because if it were not but for the grace of God, we would be in the same condition.

13

Purpose Is Spiritual

We should walk not after the flesh, but after the spirit.
Romans 8:1

The Bible was written that our joy may be complete. We can have joy, even when all is not well. When we know and believe God's Word, our joy can be full because of our faith in the reliability of His Word. Weeping may endure for a night, but joy comes in the morning (Psalm 30:5). No matter how great our trials and tribulations may be, when we trust God, we know there is a bright light at the end of every tunnel.

The joy of the Lord is not controlled by negative circumstances but by the mighty God Himself, who knows how much we can bear. He has not promised us that our lives would be free of troubles and trials, but He did assure us that He would deliver us out of them all. He is our refuge, and He is our strength—a very present help in the times of trouble (Psalm 46:1).

Life would be miserable if we wallowed in the many disparities that may come in our lifetime. Be assured that for every problem, God has a solution. Why should we stay in the valley of despair when God is there to uplift and deliver us? The Apostle Paul said, "I have learned to be content and satisfied in whatever state that I am in. I have learned to abound and I have learned to abase. Therefore, in all things I give thanks" (Philippians 4:11–12).

God gave His only begotten Son that we may daily be free from the horrific consequences of our adversary, Satan. God's love gives us life at its best, not only on this earth but also eternally in heaven. Jesus taught His disciples to pray that God's will for them be done on earth, even as it is in heaven. We should not limit ourselves to the temporary worldly joys of this life. "If we have joy in this world only, we will be men and women most miserable" (1 Corinthians 15:19). Life becomes more meaningful when our pleasures are God-centered. Our greatest joy should be the joy of our new birth in Christ. We can refer to this joy as our *born-again joy*.

Purpose is a daily pursuit. It is a destiny and a journey. This should be our daily petition as we seek God's guidance in all of our endeavors. Prayer and purpose are inseparable. Daily prayer helps us to maintain direction in the course of our daily walk with God. Each day I realize how dependent we should be on God's guidance and protection. This is not a sign of human weakness but an attribute of divine strength. Even the most astute and affluent of us must come to grips with the fact that our greatest purpose is to keep our focus on our all-sufficient source, Jesus Christ.

Each year our church is blessed with a prophetic theme on the first day of the year. The whole church embraces this prophetic vision that God has laid on my heart. These statements give us spiritual goals for the New Year that include God's blessings, God's favor, and our allegiance to please God at a greater level. The first year's theme was in 1995.

Church Prophetic Themes

1995	*Occupy until He Comes!*
1996	*He Shall Perform That Which He Has Begun!*
1997	*Your Best Is Yet to Come!*
1998	*Celebrating Our Year of Jubilee!*
1999	*Our Year of Exploits!*
2000	*Our Year of Endless Possibilities!*
2001	*Go Ye Up and Prosper, Go Ye Up and Be Blessed!*
2002	*Increasing with Christ without End!*
2003	*Arise and Experience God's Best!*

2004   *Experiencing God's Exceptional Blessings!*
2005   *Our Year to Receive God's Abundant Outpour!*
2006   *Be Blessed with God's Enormous Favor!*
2007   *Greatly Prosper, Be Healthy, and Glorify God!*
2008   *Overwhelming Blessings, Great Joy, and Great Praise!*
2009   *The Fullness of Favor and Miraculous Change!*
2010   *God's Excellent Favor and Bountiful Blessings!*
2011   *Amazing Increase, Amazing Worship, and Amazing Praise!*
2012   *Marvelous Faith, Prosperity, and Total Victory!*
2013   *Multiply in God's Goodness, God's Love, and God's Grace!*
2014   *Excel in Great Favor and Blessings of the Whole Truth!*

These prophetic statements promote us as individuals and as a church to live the abundant life at a greater level. Every year when we bring in the New Year, it promotes us to live a goal-centered life. "Without a vision, we will perish" (Proverbs 24:8). God will always bless our goodwill to succeed as we give Him the glory and the honor. We believe that as we walk with God to seek the better things in life, we will find them. And when we knock, doors will be opened unto us.

Purpose always brings fulfillment. This fulfillment gives a sense of divine significance. We should never expect others to do for us what we should be doing for ourselves. When we know our own self-worth, we are significantly more optimistic, and when we are sure about who we are, we are more likely to set goals and successfully accomplish great things. God has made it possible for each and every one of us to overcome all obstacles that may hinder this process.

My son Jimmie Jr. has often shared with me the great challenges he has faced in becoming a successful physician. This road was not paved with a bed of roses. His hard-learned lessons were through interaction with both kind and unkind people. He recently said to me, "Dad, the negative people and the hardships along the way have made me a better person and a better doctor."

Purpose motivates us to persevere, in spite of betrayals and deceptions. Sometimes this can be hard to bear, when you are deceived by those you once thought of as friends. I experienced this as a schoolteacher.

As a teacher, I always gave my best in helping children to learn. My administrators always gave me superb evaluations, but I once had an encounter with an administrator that resulted in a very unpleasant experience. Although I was told I was doing an excellent job, her actions did not always reflect this. I found it inappropriate when she referred to me as a "good Black teacher," as if she was insinuating that it was not possible to be a Black person and a good teacher. I refuse to be praised at the expense of demeaning my race or any other race. I also learned that she was sowing seeds of discord among the faculty and staff. It seems as though her ploy was to exalt herself by manipulating and dividing us. She even tried to take advantage of my strong disciplinary skills to illegally do her job in disciplining difficult students.

The general atmosphere of the whole school became so terrible that I went home, fell to my knees, and prayed that God would bring peace and justice. A few days later, I was saddened with the news that this administrator had been fired as principal. Later, she was given a job of lesser status in the school system. I felt very sorry for her. Many times after that, I would see her in public places, and it was amazing the kindness I showed her because of the God that is in me. From this experience, I learned how to overcome evil with good and triumph.

I always find peace when doing good to those who in any way may render evil toward me. We become good examples to others when we demonstrate this Christ-like behavior. I have won many sisters and brothers to Christ. Fulfilling God's purpose is manifold and lifelong. As we seek His will, He will lead us in the path of righteousness all the days of our life. As we are moved by the hand of God, day by day, goodness and mercy will follow us all the days of our lives, and we will dwell in the house of the Lord forever (Psalm 23:6).

Our individual purpose helps to define who we are.

The more we know about our purpose, the more complete and fulfilled our lives will be. We are not separate from our purpose. Every moment of our lives can be blessed by God's predestined choice for us as we seek His direction. Uniquely, all of us are missionaries. We were born to accomplish a mission that is full of endless possibilities.

14

Purpose Is about People

As I have loved you, love you also one another.
John 13:34

Every one of us has a purpose that connects us in some way to benefit others. Those of us who allow God to use us to touch others are always specially blessed by the hand of God. It is amazing how God can use even the least among us to make an enormous difference in someone's life.

A very fruitful story in Luke 10:30–34 is of the Good Samaritan. A certain man was robbed, beaten, and left to die on Jericho Road. A priest and a Levite passed by and did not offer this man any help. But a certain Samaritan came by and nursed the man's wounds and brought him to a shelter and paid all of his expenses so that he might be taken care of. Although the priest and the Levite were the highest rank in the religious world, they did not have compassion for this man. However, the Good Samaritan, who was perceived in society as a second-class citizen because of his mixed racial status, offered this man Christ-like service. This story teaches us how we are responsible for one another's welfare and how God can use common people to demonstrate the greatest form of His love. As this Good Samaritan so lovingly assisted this unfortunate man, we likewise should show Christ's love to our fellow man every day.

Each person is uniquely designed by the hand of God to be special. Even identical twins are distinctly different, regardless of how much they have in common. We are all blessed to have our own distinction as we uniquely differ in personality. This is why it is important to allow children to develop as individuals, rather than try to mold them into our own work of art. However, children need our guidance, mentorship, counsel, and direction in life. It is our responsibility to make our generations well aware that there is an absolute right and wrong and a distinguished difference between good and evil. We should be sure to emphasize to our future generations that truth is concrete.

Oftentimes, our generation will need our input and influence in their decisions concerning career, courtship, marriage and, most of all, spiritual guidance.

It is important that we demonstrate good precepts and examples. We are trailblazers and the salt of the earth for the next generation. As parents, we should heed to Proverbs 22:6. "Train up our children in the way they should go and it will not depart from them."

God has wonderful plans for each of us. As it is best stated in the song, "The safest place in the whole wide world in is in the will of God." The will of God for all of us is to obey and keep the standards in life that coincide with His commandments. Ecclesiastes 12:13 reads, "Let us hear the conclusion of the whole matter; fear God and keep His commandments for this is the whole duty of man." The "fear of God" is to highly respect God, to keep His commandments, and to obey His Word.

This is the will and divine purpose that God has designed for us all. I am convinced that all who seek the way of God and hunger and thirst after righteousness, without a doubt will always find it. We should make choices that will yield positive outcomes to our youth and the future aspects of their lives.

Positive self-esteem is very healthy. Many problems of adulthood stem from childhood insecurities. We can promote positive self-esteem without promoting arrogance and pride. A good self-image and individual confidence can contribute to success and productivity. Our faith in God can activate positive thinking about our own self-worth. We produce what we think. "So as a man thinks, so is he" (Proverbs 23:7). This is why we should be positive in our interaction in all of our human relationships, especially with children.

It is amazing how even children from good homes can battle with feelings of insecurity and poor self-esteem. Parents should give their children good and wholesome values of self-worth, using biblical principles as a foundation. Deuteronomy 6:7 reads, "And you shall diligently teach these biblical principles to your children, and talk of them when they sit in your house, and when they walk by the way, and when they lie down, and when they rise up." Consistent, affirmative, Bible-based self-esteem should be religiously instilled in our young people.

Purpose is manifold in that it fulfills the needs of the whole person. Our total purpose is to live a Christ-like lifestyle, 365 days a year, seven days a week, and all twenty-four hours of the day. As we fulfill our purpose, we fulfill our need to live the abundant life. We all need to feel needed. There is an inborn space in each of our hearts that causes us to yearn for our God-given reason for existence.

It is important that we not deceive ourselves with distractions in life that deter us from the things that really matter. Again, what we *should* do with our lives and what we *want* to do with our lives can be completely different. However, when we become submissive to the Word of God, it becomes a joy to *want to do what we should do* in our daily lives.

All of us have a need to fulfill our desire to accomplish goals in life. When we have a vision for our lives, we are motivated to succeed. It is then that the things we want and need are uniquely fulfilled. No monetary value can replace the intensity of joy and contentment of the internal sense of our God-given fulfillment.

Throughout our lives, we need to be focused on the things that are most important. Too often, even the most disciplined people are tempted to lose their focus. I remember Missionary Mary Harris who spent many years ministering to the impoverished community of Liberia, West Africa. Missionary Harris often told us that she had been asked many times how she liked her work as a missionary. She responded by rhetorically asking, "How do I like it? It doesn't make any difference how much I like it. God called me to do this work, and I know I must do it. I enjoy doing any and everything that God wants me to do. I never stopped to think whether I like it or not. It doesn't make any difference. Whether and wherever the Lord says go, I go, and where He says to stay, I stay."

I always chuckle when I think of how simple but wise she was in thinking so seriously about her divine call.

Many times, divine purpose takes us out of our comfort zone, but it will lead to inner contentment and priceless peace. Moses said, "I'd rather suffer with the people of God than to enjoy the pleasures of sin for a season" (Hebrews 11:25).

Nothing happens by accident; not even those events that appear to haphazardly happen. All things work together for the good of all of us who have been redeemed. Sometimes bad things happen to good people. However, bad things should not discourage or deter our character and behavior.

The story of Job is a perfect example of the demonstration of this wisdom. Job was indeed a perfect and upright man, yet he experienced some of the worst trials and tribulations. However, he never blamed or became bitter toward God. When he was overwhelmed with some of the worst misfortunes in life, he cried out to God and said, "Although it seems like you are slaying me, I will still trust you" (Job 13:15). With this kind of attitude, Job overcame insurmountable adversities that strongly attacked him. It is very obvious that Job was determined to demonstrate perseverance, in spite of the daring hardships in his life. Therefore, the latter of Job's life turned out better for him by far. Likewise, we should allow our faith in God's promises to be more powerful than our trials and tribulations.

Remember, God is in control. Jesus said, "Be of good cheer; I have overcome the world for you" (John 16:33). So remember there is hope in the midst of every storm. "Weeping may endure for a night, but joy comes in the morning" (Psalm 30:5).

You are not an accident. When God created you, He definitely had something special in mind. God had a special purpose for you, even before you were born. In His sovereign will, He preplanned your special destiny. Therefore, it is very important that much prayer and thought be given to such questions as, "What is my purpose in life? Am I fulfilling God's purpose? How can I do it more effectively?" Purpose is supernatural.

As it reads in Matthew 6:33, when we first seek the kingdom of God and His righteousness, all the other things we may desire will be added unto us. It is very important that we depend on God in our daily decision making. We should follow Him as He leads us in the path of righteousness, but we should never try to take the lead. We should allow Him to lead because the steps of a good man or good woman are ordered by the Lord (Psalm 37:23).

God has never done anything without your best interest in mind. He has a special and blessed design for each and every human being. God can even reverse the unfortunate things that happen in our lives. Many of my personal experiences have proven it to be so. Many of us have been in relationships where we experienced disappointment, but we can even learn through disappointing experiences.

The older we get, the wiser we should become. Sometimes God's choice can conflict with our choice. There is a difference between what we need and what we want. I believe that even after much prayer and serious consideration, we should be patient in making choices. Serious choices should always be made according to the will of God. Serious decisions should be made patiently, prayerfully, and thoughtfully. Sometimes we can make decisions that lead to heartbreaking consequences, which can negatively affect generations after we are gone.

Fulfilling our purpose can be trying and challenging. Jesus demonstrated this many times. He spent thirty-three years on earth, and many of these years were filled with the challenges of trying to help those who refused to receive the endless benefits of His desire to help them.

The most painful experience was the agony and brutality Jesus experienced at the time of His crucifixion and death. He, like all human beings, dreaded the horror of the dire suffering and human torture that was required to atone our sins. Jesus totally submitted Himself to the will of God as He looked to heaven and said, "Not my will but thy will be done" (Luke 22:42). His obedience gave the whole world hope, life, and everlasting life. Had Jesus not died, we would all be most miserable. He became poor that we may become rich. He became sin that we may be righteous. He died that we may live. He became a man of sorrow that we may be filled with the fullness of joy.

It is very encouraging to know that Jesus can relate to our pain, hurts, trials, and tribulations, as He was acquainted with these experiences Himself. As Jesus suffered in the flesh, we also shall be prepared to do likewise. He said, "If we suffer with Him, we shall also reign with Him" (2 Timothy 2:12).

I can recall how I have served my purpose in shepherding my flock. I have uniquely experienced the pain of wanting more for many individuals than they wanted for themselves. I have never become discouraged in my efforts to help people. I have never given up on an individual. I am convinced that God called, anointed, and appointed me to love and serve all people, regardless of their circumstances. Unfortunately, my passion to love has not always been easy. In fact, it has sometimes caused much suffering. As the Word of God states, "Love suffers long" (1 Corinthians 13:4).

I am grateful to be blessed with the gift of longsuffering. I have experienced being hurt, betrayed, and deceived by some of those I have loved and sacrificed for the most. Sometimes this has become overwhelming and trying to my flesh. Pastors are also human. Jesus Himself became human that He may be our example and demonstrate how to love and serve in spite of disappointments. Jesus said, "But I say unto you, love your enemies, bless them that curse you, do good to them that hate you, and pray for them that despitefully use you and persecute you" (Matthew 5:44).

I have learned that we can love our enemy with the kind of love that transforms them into our friends. I believe that God has given me a special gift to do this. To love everyone is a benefit and a privilege, not a duty.

When we are faced with opposition, we should never seek to retaliate but always conquer by a willingness to forgive those who may trespass against us. Love conquers all, and the power of love will always win. Without purpose or vision, life is meaningless. Without God's divine guidance, we would be like ships without sails, airplanes without wings, and cars without engines. Often I think of how brief our lives are on this earth and how important it is that we redeem the time. We should never take our daily blessings from the Lord for granted. Our time here on this earth is too short to live carelessly.

Now that our three children are grown, I look back and think of how fast they grew up. My wife and I are so happy that we invested the best that we had to offer in them, with all our passion and perseverance. We have no regrets in rearing our children. We did all we knew to do and gave all we had with God's guidance that they might be enormously blessed and prosperous in this life and the life to come. We gave all of them the tools they need to successfully raise their children in the same godly fashion in which they were reared. We taught them to do their best and to give their best that they, through their contributions, can make the world a better place.

We will always treasure some very special memories as a family. Christmas was always one of the most joyous times of the year. Decorating the Christmas tree always filled our hearts with special memories. Jimmie Jr. and Avery always went with me to pick out a Christmas tree, while Faith chose to stay home and prepare the decorations and ornaments. Our favorite ornaments are the picture frame ornaments of past memories that we hang on the tree.

Enjoying family at all seasons of the year should be a part of every family's purpose. Joy and happiness are the plan of God for our lives. We should plan to be happy. Therefore, take pleasure in the virtue of showing kindness to all mankind.

Back Row - Jimmie Horton Jr., Jimmie Horton Sr., Avery Horton
Front Row - Faith Horton & Michelle Horton

Lady Michelle Horton & Bishop Jimmie R. Horton Sr.

Clockwise from left - Bishop Jimmie R. Horton, Rev. Monte Asbury, Lady Michelle Horton, Hannah Horton, Eleanor Horton, Jimmie Horton Jr., Laura Asbury, & Avery Horton, Lucas Asbury & Faith Horton in background Celebrating Eleanor's (Ellie) Christening

*Jimmie R. Horton Sr.
High School--seventeen years old*

Back Row - Jimmie, Roy, Eddie, Mother Mattie,
Daddy Joshua, David, Lindsey, Arthur
Front Row - Dorothy, Isabella, Ann, Mattie and Barbara

Daddy Joshua Horton & Mother Mattie Horton

Joshua & Mattie Horton's 75th Wedding Anniversary

Polished performance

Joshua Horton, 71, the shoeshine man at the Walthall Hotel for 10 years, takes a lunch break

Morris & Emily Horton (Paternal Grandparents)

Ed Lloyd (Maternal Grandfather)

Ella Brow-Tyner—Paternal Great-Grandmother

My oldest known ancestry can be traced back to my paternal great-grandmother, Ella Brow-Tyner, who was my grandmother Emily's mother. She was married to Richard Tyner. She was born into slavery in Hazlehurst, Mississippi, in 1845 and passed away in 1902. We were very fortunate to find her picture in the bottom of a trunk of my grandmother Emily's memoirs. Her picture portrays strength, dignity, wisdom, and courage. Apparently, she was a well-favored and valued house slave because of her regal apparel and appearance.

Teachers to be honored

Black educators to be recognized

By John Willard
QUAD-CITY TIMES

Three retired black teachers in the Davenport School District will be saluted Saturday for their groundbreaking efforts in helping all students achieve educational excellence.

The teachers are Gloria Collins, Jimmie R. Horton and Evelyn Thompson.

They will be honored during the 11th annual banquet of the Parmenas Benevolent Association Inc. of Hiram Lodge No. 19, Free & Accepted Masons, and Naomi Chapter No. 1, Order of the Eastern Star, both affiliated with the Prince Hall Grand Lodge.

The banquet will be held at the Clarion Hotel, 5002 N. Brady St., Davenport, with hospitality hour from 6-7 p.m. and dinner at 7 p.m. The donation is $30 a person.

The two lodges began recognizing African-American teachers during their annual banquet last year, and they plan to make it a tradition. Black teachers not only have served as role models for black students, but their presence helps all children by exposing them to other cultures, organizers said.

"We feel that it is good that our children and grandchildren have the privilege of having black teachers. We want these educators to know that they have done a great job," said banquet chairman Alberta Crump, who attended Davenport schools before the first black teachers were hired in the 1950s and 1960s.

Gloria Collins

Gloria Collins parlayed her passion for music into a 34-year teaching career at Jefferson Elementary and Wood Intermediate schools.

Her own music studies might have been derailed, though, if her mother had not bucked her high school counselor.

Retired teacher and counselor Jimmie R. Horton spent 15 years at Lincoln Fundamental School in Davenport during a 25-year teaching career in Davenport schools. He also founded Gospel Mission Church, Davenport, where he has served as pastor for 22 years.

Bishop Horton at Lincoln School, where he taught most of his 25 years in the Davenport Community School District

Quad-City Times

TUESDAY, APRIL 19, 2011 • 75 CENTS

CIVIL RIGHTS MARCH REMEMBERED

Davenport Mayor Bill Gluba, left, and Bishop Jimmie Horton of the Gospel Mission Temple lead a group marching Monday to re-enact a civil rights gathering in August 1963. Later, a plaque marking the event was unveiled at St. Anthony's Church in Davenport, one of seven points of interest on Davenport's new Civil Rights History Walking Tour.

Jeff Cook/QUAD-CITY TIMES

Front Clockwise from Left - Davenport Mayor Gluba and Bishop Jimmie Horton of the Gospel Mission Temple lead a group marching Monday to reenact a civil rights gathering in August 1983. Later, a plaque marking the event was unveiled at St. Anthony's Church in Davenport, one of seven points of interest on Davenport's new Civil Rights History Walking Tour.

Gospel Mission Temple
The outside view of the spacious edifice
built on 35 prime acres of land

The inside view of the elegant spacious
sanctuary of Gospel Mission Temple

15

Don't Major in the Minors

What does it profit to gain the whole world and lose your soul?
Matthew 16:26

The older I get, the more I learn to live and make each day really count. I am now what society calls a senior citizen, and I feel as healthy as when I was in my early youth. However, I constantly remind myself how important it is that I redeem the time. It is important that we all do the best we can, while we can.

It is very important to me that God be first in every area of my life, especially with family and church. This is the foundation and focus of my passion as I serve others. I often say that before we can help others, we must first be loyal to ourselves, to our family, and to our home. We must follow the pattern of the wisdom of God's Word that admonishes us to prioritize the order of our choices.

We should constantly guard against spending too much time involving ourselves with concerns that are of lesser importance. Life on this earth is too short. Our mission is too great, and our time is too valuable to waste. The Word of God states, "We should work while it is day, for the night is coming when no one can work" (John 9:4).

Eternity is serious. Everything that we do affects our destiny and our eternity. As I think back over my life, I am amazed at how so many of my acquaintances, friends, and family have gone into the judgment, never to pass this way again. Unfortunately, some of them did not triumphantly live life to the fullest. They left this world with so many loose ends. Some even died what I would call an *untimely death*. This is to say that they not only died before their time, but they did not use the time they had very wisely.

Not only have I learned by my mistakes, but I have learned by other's mistakes, as well. As human beings, we are all tempted to do some things that seem good to us but are not good *for* us. We, at all times, need to be aware of the consequences of our actions, whether profitable or unprofitable. Sometimes we reap consequences not only of the things we have done but of the things we should have done. Therefore, we should live our lives thoughtfully and circumspectly each day, giving much thought to our decisions before putting them into action. As the old saying goes, "Always look before you leap." All serious decisions should be preceded by prayer and meditation.

To major in the majors requires a life of temperance. One of the greatest blessings in life is to possess the gift of controlling one's self, according to the Word of God. The power to control and discipline oneself has endless benefits. The lack of ability to moderate or control our human will is extremely dangerous.

Moderation and control is of extreme importance in every facet of our lives. As it is healthy for us to have a good appetite for natural food, it is necessary that we control what we eat and how much we eat. Not considering this fact can cause detrimental consequences. Control and moderation in other areas of our lives are mandatory for healthy living as well.

At some point in our lives, we have all experienced the temptation of taking inappropriate action during moments of anger. As we have matured as Christians, we have gained better control of our temperament. The Word of the Lord says, "Be angry but sin not" (Ephesians 4:26). As we must control our temperament of anger, we likewise should take full control over our strong passions.

One of the strongest passions of the human body is that of our sexual desires. It is a blessing to have a healthy sexual desire for the opposite sex; however, it must be fulfilled within God's plan of sexuality. "There is no temptation given unto us whereby God has not given us the proper way to deal with it" (1 Corinthians 10:13). Therefore, we must demonstrate to the world that we can make decisions that will help others to be motivated to make life-giving decisions, rather than decisions that may yield detrimental consequences.

I can recall a decision I made which, even to this day, has a great impact on my life. As a young man in high school, I met a young lady at the state choir festival. After dating for a short time, we became more attracted to one another.

During those times, we both demonstrated how our physical attraction could be controlled with common sense and strong ethical principles. She even verbalized to me how my temptation was obvious to her but how she admired my demonstration of self-control. She said that I possessed the quality of a strong man. The Bible gives us clear admonition with the Scripture that reads, "Flee youthful lust" (2 Timothy 2:22). I am enjoying great dividends today because of the wise decisions I made in my youth to respect all women as vessels of honor.

Conquering youthful passions will yield lifelong natural and spiritual benefits. My parents instilled these wise and healthy choices in me. They taught me that in respecting the virtue of all women, I empower my own self-respect and integrity.

Prevention is better than cure. We always reap what we sow. Clean living has endless rewards. This is not to say that we are flawless. We all, in some way, can perfect our power to control our fleshly passions. It is important we get this message across to our youth as soon as possible. They need to be constantly reminded of how dangerous, senseless games can limit the quality of leading a productive, successful, and prosperous life.

We should give our children the opportunity to learn by our mistakes. We should share with them the areas in our lives in which we ourselves have made bad decisions. We should confess that if we had the opportunity to do it all over again, we would make better choices. We should also be examples of how we ourselves have learned from our own mistakes. We improve life for all when we improve our next generation.

One of my greatest motivations is the words that my father often said to me: "Son, I want you to do better than I did." He never seemed intimidated by my obtaining higher levels of status in education or any other part of my life. He often taught us to pursue and stand up for the right so that we may always come out on top.

We were taught the importance of treating everyone respectfully. Dad and Mom often showed us how to be respectful, even when we are confronted disrespectfully. During the fall of 1968, my brother Lindsey and I helped our dad clean Mr. Glover's office building. On Thanksgiving Day, Mr. Glover came to our house with quails that he wanted my mother to clean and dress for him. In a very disrespectful way, he asked me if my mother was home because he wanted her to clean the birds for him immediately. I responded by saying, "Yes, Mother is home, but she will not be cleaning those birds for you. Today is Thanksgiving." He left hurriedly, and I never saw him again. I am sure he must have told my father of this incident, but Dad never rebuked me. I still remember the good feeling that I had because I did not behave disrespectfully in that situation.

My father refused to work in the office again. He taught us to forgive and rise above hate and overcome evil with good. My father never fit into the "Uncle Tom" system. He never accepted the Jim Crow atmosphere that stagnated healthy human relations in the South.

I was a senior in high school the year that Dr. Martin Luther King Jr. was assassinated. It was like a horrible dream. I very vividly remember our principal announcing on the intercom system at school. "It is with much regret that I inform the faculty, staff, and student body that Dr. Martin Luther King Jr. has been assassinated." Many of the faculty and student body were so shocked and filled with grief that they were overcome with uncontrollable emotions and had to be excused from school for the day.

The dark cloud of grief that hung over our community and nation seemed endless.

Dr. King's assassination caused many racial riots to break out on college campuses and neighborhoods. These riots continued into the early 1970s on college campuses all over the nation. The riot that broke out in spring 1970 on the campus of Jackson State was very traumatic. The National Guard opened fire, leaving hundreds of bullet holes in the women's dormitory. Two young men lost their lives, and several students were injured. This incident caused restlessness in the city of Jackson, the nation, and the world. The National Association for the Advancement of Colored People (NAACP) held large gatherings and town meetings to address this bigotry and racism.

It was during my high school and college years that I became infused with a passion to contend for equal rights. I became interested in reading and researching the lives of trailblazers and pioneers of the Civil Rights Movement. I sought to learn more about the nonviolent philosophers, such as Dr. Martin Luther King Jr. I studied Malcolm X, Harriet Tubman, W. E. B. Dubois, Frederick Douglas, Rosa Parks, Fannie Lou Hamer, Sojourner Truth, Mary McLeod Bethune, Medgar Evers, Richard Wright, Bishop Richard Allen, Bishop Charles Price Jones, Bishop Charles Harrison Mason, John F. Kennedy, Jesse Jackson, James Weldon Johnson, John Rosamond Johnson,

Bishop Arthur M. Brazier and, of course, the Reverend Joshua Horton. I have always had a burning desire to see all people treated fairly. We were taught that hate is poisonous, destructive, and deadly. Each member of society has an important role in taking a militant stand against injustice; especially the church leaders.

Jesus militantly objected to bigotry and inequality. He emphatically stated that to have respect of person is sin. He also said, "What we do unto the least, we have done unto Him" (Matthew 25:40). Jesus demonstrated love to all people. He gave His life for the whole world so that nobody would be lost but accept Him as their Savior and forever live in heaven with Him.

A great Bible story is when Jesus converted the prejudiced Samaritan woman at the well. He asked her for a drink of water, but she refused Him because He was a Jew. He showed her His great love by offering her the water of the Spirit. He said, "Woman, if you drink of my water, there shall be in you a well springing up unto salvation and everlasting life" (John 4:14). It was apparent that she accepted His offer, because she ran into the city and invited others to come and meet this man named Jesus.

I have always enjoyed the Negro spirituals, hymns, and folk songs of the early revolution of the Civil Rights Movement, such as "We Shall Overcome":

LIVE THE UNLIMITED LIFE

We shall overcome.
We shall overcome.
We shall overcome someday.
Oh deep in my heart, I do believe,
We shall overcome some day.

Another of my favorites is the "Negro National Anthem," by James Weldon Johnson and John Rosamond Johnson:

Lift every voice and sing,
'Til earth and heaven ring,
Ring with the harmonies of liberty.
Let our rejoicing rise,
High as the listening skies.
Let it resound loud as the rolling sea.

In 2008, I was appointed by the mayor of Davenport, Iowa, to serve on the Affirmative Action Commission for the city of Davenport. Serving on this commission has allowed me to become more involved with a diverse group of city officials and community leaders. This experience has broadened my perception of the social and economic needs in our city, nation, and world as we place emphasis on equality and justice for all citizens. In my collaboration with church and community leaders, we all agree that it is time to take a stand as never before against the social acts of bigotry of all forms.

Other spirituals I enjoy are "Swing Low, Sweet Chariot," "Steal Away," and "Keep Inching Along."

I enjoyed the poetry of Maya Angelou, Langston Hughes, Richard Wright, Margaret Walker Alexander, Phyllis Wheatley, Paul Lawrence Dunbar, and James Baldwin. These prolific writers militantly and poetically protested against the evils of bigotry in America. Margaret Walker Alexander made this very clear in her poem, "For My People." Likewise, so did Sojourner Truth in her speech, "Ain't I a Woman?" Fannie Lou Hamer so eloquently opposed the oppression of people of color in America in her speech, "Is This America?," as she addressed the National Democratic Convention on August 2, 1964.

The African American pulpit has always been a powerful influence in speaking for many who could not speak for themselves. The Black preacher often uses the biblical story of how God sent Moses to tell Pharaoh to let His people Israel go, as an example of God's strong passion to execute equality for all people. Martin Luther King Jr. often reminded racist America of her sins and admonished her to repent. He often said, "America, it is time that you repent of the sins that you have committed for many years against your Black brother. Although you have not shown us love, we still are going to love you." He often said, "Injustice anywhere is a threat to justice everywhere." In our fight and plight for civil rights, we must consider the importance of how we must be inclusive of all people.

It has become very obvious that police officers across our nation are more apt to stop cars that are driven by Blacks than Whites. We have taken measures to stop police harassment against the Black youth. Many times, they have been unjustifiably pulled over and questioned by these officers. These acts must be taken into consideration and acted upon. I am convinced that injustice and racism to some degree will always exist, but we must never accept it. We must consistently fight to minimize this illness of society. We should fight until judgment runs down like water and righteousness runs down like a mighty stream (Amos 5:24).

I learned the first lessons of the importance of civil rights and human justice from my father. He was indeed a spiritual and social activist who took a stand against inequality. He often told us that he wanted each of us to excel and be treated fairly. He also taught us that we should love and respect everyone but to never accept any form of discrimination. It is amazing how we were a very functional family in such a dysfunctional social system of Black America. In spite of the system, we were taught survival.

I take great pleasure in emphasizing the importance of a solid family structure. I take my responsibilities and obligations as a husband and a father in my home very seriously. If a man cannot properly care for his wife and children, he cannot adequately serve in any other capacity of society, especially in the house of God. It is more important to demonstrate love than to merely talk about love. My father often said, "Charity begins at home and then spreads abroad."

As I reminisce over my childhood and youth, I am amazed. We were the richest poor people ever. We had little material goods but plenty of everything that we needed most. I recently found an article from the *Jackson Clarion Ledger*, featuring my father, titled "Polished Performance." The photo of my dad in this article looked like a classic *National Geographic* feature. He apparently was taking his lunch break while seated by his shoeshine stand, eating a sandwich. This photo depicted the sum total of my father's humble means of making a living. It was a perfect reflection of his dignity, integrity, and serious character. The message of this photograph still lingers in my mind.

Dad was never too proud to labor six days a week in order to support his family. He did this for many years. It reminded me of the Scripture, "He that humbles himself shall be exalted" (Matthew 23:12). Dad was an educator in the school of divine wisdom, knowledge, and understanding. He and Mother majored in the majors. Life to them was about investing in the things that pertained to God, their marriage, family, and devotion to others. They are a living legacy of the perfect example of the foundation of a functional family.

Our lives are spent as a tale being told. As individuals, we play a major role in writing our own script. I often think of how God puts choices in our hands, and we must make the right one. As stated in the Word, God said, "I set before you blessings and curses. Choose you this day whom you will serve" (Joshua 24:15). We are blessed to have the privilege to reverse bad choices.

Even in the area of our personal devotion to God, we receive at the level that we give. Our devotion to God serves a paramount place in determining our level of success in life. When we worship and praise Him graciously with our best devotion, He responds with great favor. It is very apparent to me that God delights in working mighty wonders and miracles in our daily lives. It is a blessing to experience the health and wealth of consistently serving the Lord. One of the major purposes of each of our lives should be to make an indelible mark in someone's life and to improve his or her life as often as we can. I have been remarkably blessed to have been touched by the lives of many.

I developed a close relationship with seniors in my family, especially my father's brothers and sisters. I will always be grateful for my Aunt Estella, Aunt Bea, Aunt Carrie, and Aunt Anna. In my junior and senior year in high school, I developed a close relationship with my Aunt Anna. She was a unique woman who had strong Indian features.

I spent many days and nights at Aunt Anna's house in 1967 and 1968. She often gave quotes from her accumulation of superstitious folklore. Before she was enlightened, she spent too much time dwelling on these mystical beliefs. Many of her decisions were affected by the folklore and superstitious practices that she heard from individuals during her youth. She thought it would bring bad luck if a female was the first visitor on a Monday morning. For this reason, a woman was never welcome at her house on Monday mornings.

Aunt Anna also believed it was bad luck to laugh too much in the morning because "too much laughter in the morning will always lead to some form of sorrow before sundown." Other quotes from her collection were "It is a long o' lane that has no end and a bad o' wind that never changes, and the pitcher may go to the well many times, but one day, it will soon break."

She loved me dearly. I often prayed she would be free from the bondages of these superstitions, and God answered my prayers. She went to be with the Lord, free and full of grace and faith in God.

Aunt Estella was the first of Dad's sisters whom my siblings and I met. She never missed a summer in coming to see us. Every time I see a passenger train, I think of Aunt Estella because she would take the *City of New Orleans* Amtrak train to see us every summer. She brought a lot of joy with her.

Aunt Estella was a devout Pentecostal woman. Her conversations were generally centered on the miraculous power of God to save and heal. She often told the story of how she was healed of terminal cancer at the age of thirty. She lived to be almost ninety years old. I will always treasure the unity and dedication she demonstrated in encouraging us to keep strong family ties.

Aunt Bea also had a significant influence upon my life. She was a true Apostolic woman. Her greatest joy was to assist in helping individuals who wanted to receive the baptism in the Holy Spirit. She was strongly enthusiastic about the empowerment of the Holy Ghost and would always tell others that God could fill them with the Holy Ghost right in the place where they were standing or sitting.

Aunt Carrie was a unique character in her own right. I will always treasure the days and nights I spent at her house on St. Lawrence Street near Seventy-Ninth

Street in Chicago. I enjoyed the Saturday morning rides we took downtown on the elevated train. We would have desserts of frozen strawberries at the downtown Walgreen's drugstore. In the early '40s, Aunt Carrie left for Chicago and gave all the contents of her house at 223 Clifton Street to my parents. As I stated earlier, I was born in that little house. I will always remember her for the good times we shared together in church and how we would eat at the soul-food restaurant, Glady's, on Indiana Avenue after church.

I will treasure the precious memories of attending Aunt Estella and Aunt Bea's churches. Aunt Estella's church was held on Sunday mornings at Wendell Phillips High School. The Reverend Williams Freeman was her pastor. He was also a very interesting character. He was a tall, Caucasian man with a mystical persona.

The services were very informal and seasoned with a Pentecostal atmosphere. Reverend Freeman emphasized the divine healing power of God. Aunt Bea's church was Apostolic, with a more organized and formal structure. I enjoyed the beautiful music and impressive choir. The members of my aunts' churches were very fond of me. My exposure to their churches and my home church had a great influence upon my ministry. Both our natural and spiritual experiences together help to greatly mold and shape our lives.

Our good and bad experiences have purpose. Our family's great, spiritual legacy is amazing. One of my greatest gifts is my ancestry. All family ancestries have both positive and negative attributes. We should choose to embrace the positives and reverse the negatives. I am very fortunate to have more positive than negative features to recall of my ancestors. The only two areas in the Horton ancestry that I felt the need to reverse are the limited education and poverty. Those two negatives have been greatly reversed by the grace and mercy of God, beginning with my generation. Poverty and limited education no longer dominate my generation.

I praise God that my wife and I both have worked hard to demonstrate to our children the importance of education. We have encouraged them to follow in our footsteps and pursue the highest level of improving themselves. Every generation should counteract the bondages of the former generations and pass on greater hope to the future generations. The more God gives us, the more we have to give to others. In spite of the adversities of our forefathers and foremothers, we owe it to them to progressively carry on that which they have passed on to us.

It is important we redeem the time and passionately utilize every moment of our lives. I often think of how swiftly time creeps upon us. I am so grateful when I evaluate the years that God has already given to me. We should have something to show for the years that we spent on this earth.

An outstanding Bible story is the one that teaches us to make good choices before making decisions in life. It tells of the man who considered a building project, but he did not count up the cost of construction and later found that he did not have enough money to finish his building project. This brought him much embarrassment, as there were many who made mockery of him. We should make every moment count and maximize every moment of each day. This should be taught to our children early in life. We should encourage them to be very selective in making serious choices.

We should also be sure to promote wholesome entertainment, rather than the low-street mentality. In our efforts to reverse this, we should seek to filter our society of its immoral and social ills. We should promote productive values in all facets of our society.

It is imperative that parents and teachers communicate the importance of role modeling healthy and positive influences to students. Many of our advanced technology improvements have been both positive and negative. For instance, our youth need to be more mobile in order to be healthy. More time should be spent engaging in physical, fun activities than in sitting at the computer for long hours, playing computer games. Cell phones have diminished a great percentage of wholesome, verbal interaction, due to frequent texting for hours throughout the day.

We conducted an open forum at our church that addressed the positives and negatives of our modern technology. It was mentioned how the cell phone is a wonderful invention, but it has its downside. Text messaging and all other messaging devices that use impersonal contact are inventions that have been a big plus in communication. However, it has contributed to less oral communication and verbal interaction, specifically among family and friends. People are simply not talking to each other as they did in the past.

It is pertinent for us to remember that nothing can take the place of the personal contact of hearing a familiar voice. Machines can never take the place of people. It can be very frustrating to interact with a mechanical voice rather than talking to a real person. Although e-mail is quite a remarkable discovery, it should never replace conversing with a live human being. We should do more to contribute to establishing and maintaining good interpersonal relationships than cold, mechanical ones.

On Sunday, March 20, 2011, I preached a sermon titled, "The One Hundredfold Blessing." The Scripture text was taken from Matthew 19:27-29. Here, Jesus speaks of how the fullness of life's blessings become a reality when we put Him first. "Verily I say unto you, that those who prefer me more than houses, brethren, sisters, father, mother, wife, children, land, for my sake will receive a hundred-fold and shall inherit eternal life" (Matthew 19:29). This powerful Scripture gives hope to every believer and nonbeliever. God always blesses us remarkably when we show Him the uttermost preference in making choices in our daily life. Jesus Himself assured Peter and the other disciples that their choice of following Him wholeheartedly would pay everlasting and enormous dividends.

The following old Negro spiritual, "Give Me Jesus," very profoundly captures the value of Jesus' first conceptions: The words are:

> In the morning when I rise, give me Jesus.
> Dark midnight was my cry, give me Jesus.
> Oh when I come to die, give me Jesus.
> You may have this whole wide world,
> But give me Jesus.

This spiritual conclusively makes it obvious that when we major in the very essence of the full identity of Jesus Christ, we are left lacking nothing. We are complete in Him, and in Him all things consist!

16

A Powerful Relationship with God

Draw close to God and He will draw close to you.
James 4:8

God spoke to Moses and said, "Give my Word to the house of Israel and say unto them, hear O Israel the Lord your God is one Lord and you shall love the Lord your God with all your heart, all your soul, and with all your strength" (Mark 12:29, 30). The intimate relationship we have with God was predestined before the world was formed. He chose us before we had the knowledge of knowing who He is. John 15:16 reads, "You have not chosen me, but I have chosen you that you should go and bring forth fruit that your fruit may remain." The closer we are to God, the greater our potential to bear good and godly fruit. These benefits are endless. God is infinite in His ability and power to richly bless us.

I am strongly convinced that true relationships are God-like relationships. I believe that God-fearing people are the only people that are trustworthy. Even the best of humanity is limited within its own human ability, but with God, all things are possible. In our weakness, He is our strength. He is our supernatural glue that holds our lives together.

What value is any relationship without God? What is a marriage without God? What is a mother, father, brother, or sister relationship without some divine intervention? God is our source of love, strength, integrity, wisdom, and understanding. His presence in our lives allows our relationship with others to have endurance and stability. It is His strong passion and desire to always stay close to us. What a privilege and opportunity it is to seek His presence more and more every day. He has given us His Word to believe and receive all of His promises. He has given us His spirit that we may never stray from His path.

All good relationships are wonderful, but our relationship with Him is most wonderful. Our passion for Him should exceed and excel our passion for anybody or anything. His presence is our access to total fulfillment of every good and wonderful thing. "If we draw nigh to God, He will likewise draw nigh to us" (James 4:8).

The old saints used to say, "If you make one step, He'll make two." In other words, if you consistently walk with God, He will consistently walk with you. I strongly believe that once we give our lives to Christ, we have spiritual security. However, I believe that just as in our natural relationships, there are stipulations that determine the quality and endurance of our relationship with God. We are just as secure in Christ, as we live according to His expectations. We are just as saved as we live. Saved is as saved does.

God's Word admonishes us that we are known by the fruit we bear. We cannot serve two masters. Jesus once said, "Why call me Lord, Lord and not do the things I say" (Luke 6:46). We cannot say that we are God's children when we live the lifestyle that displeases Him. Beware of the dangers of the deception of the doctrine that teaches false eternal security. Jesus made it possible that once we become a Christian, we can remain in Him forever. One of the attributes of the Holy Spirit is to keep us saved until the coming of our Lord.

I believe in eternal security. I know the same God that saves us is able to keep us saved, but He has given us a will to choose. Every day, we are put in a position to make those choices. Our actions reveal where we stand with God. He does not force us to give our hearts to Him or to continue to serve Him. The choice of each individual is what makes this love relationship so sweet and special. He does not force us to love Him; He only allows us to choose to love Him. A love relationship is not like a programmed disk in a computer; rather, it is like a man who desires to marry a woman who mutually desires to love and marry him in return.

It takes each individual to have a true and meaningful relationship that will endure. If one or both individuals begin to take the other for granted, the relationship suffers the possibility of deteriorating. Likewise, our relationship with God must be mutual. Jesus said, "I am the vine and you are the branches; every branch that is in me, I will purge it. However, if there is a branch in me that does not bear fruit I will cut it off and throw it in the fire" (John 15:5-6). Just that Scripture alone is evidence that if we do not bear Christ-like fruits of our salvation, we disconnect ourselves from a relationship with God. God's Word constantly reminds us of our daily commitment to walk the Christ-like walk as well as talk the Christ-like talk.

Love must be nurtured in the divine sense as it is in the human relationship. It will be foolish to say once married, always married, without fulfilling the necessary marital responsibilities and expectations. God wants us to show Him how much we love Him, just as a wife wants her husband to show her how much he loves her. It must be consistent. A glamorous wedding without a glamorous marriage is senseless. The pomp and circumstances of a glamorous wedding does not compensate for an unhappy marriage. Likewise, verbal commitment to God is to no avail when it is not actively demonstrated.

LIVE THE UNLIMITED LIFE

We must be daily devoted to Christ, just as a marriage requires devotion from both husband and wife. Good relationships require sacrifice. Good relationships require taking great pleasure in pleasing the other. If we please God, He will more than give us our heart's desires. God has feelings. He desires to be loved as much as He desires to love.

God is a jealous God. His jealousy is holy and righteous. It is the kind of jealousy that has a strong passion to protect, provide, and preserve us. His love compelled Him to have mercy upon us. Because of His love and mercy, He gave us His gift of grace. This grace, in turn, saved us.

Our faith allows us to receive His love, mercy, and grace, which saves us from all of our sins. This grace is greater than all of our sin. The songwriter Daniel B. Towner very eloquently said it when he wrote, "Marvelous Grace":

Marvelous grace of our loving Lord,
Grace that exceeds our sins and our guilt,
Yonder on Calvary's mount outpoured,
There where the blood of the lamb was spilt.
Grace, grace, God's grace,
Grace that will pardon and cleanse within,
Grace, grace, God's grace,
Grace that is greater than all our sin.

Our relationship with God is empowered by our daily interaction with Him. We should never take His grace for granted. Grace is not our ticket to sin without paying the penalty. The penalty of sin from the garden of Eden, even to the present day, is a great price. The price of sin was so great that the blood of Jesus was the only acceptable sacrifice of atonement. We were not purchased with corruptible things as silver and gold but by the precious blood of Jesus (1 Peter 1:18). Since the penalty of sin was paid at the cost of Jesus' giving His life, we, like God, should hate all evil and seek to please Him.

Sin is horrible. Therefore, every generation should take precaution in taking a stand against promiscuous lifestyles. We should pass a righteous lineage, not a lineage contaminated with that which God hates most. For this reason, every individual should seek to pursue his or her best in life and never blame past generations. Every present generation should improve the misfortune of the past generation, to improve the future generation.

As an African American male, I have sought to do all that I can to reverse many of the negative stereotypes of our people. I believe I can continually make a noticeable difference in influencing our youth to lead more productive lives. Our hope for social change has a divine solution. "Blessed is the nation whose God is the Lord" (Psalms 33:12).

On April 19, 2011, I participated in a reenactment of the 1963 March on Washington. The following day, tears almost came to my eyes when I saw a picture of myself in the morning paper, marching with Mayor Bill Gluba. I began to reminisce as I thought of the progress our human race has made since that first march on Washington in August 1963. I had flashbacks of the horrible struggles of the past, but I was also filled with hope, knowing that God will help us to fight our battles, as we have yet much to overcome.

Much of our progress can be attributed to the prayers of the old slaves, saints, and patriots of the church and the Civil Rights Movements. Much can be attributed to the preachers, abolitionists, and martyrs who have gone on to receive their due reward. Their strong faith and fortitude has served their most holy and sacred mission of bringing justice and peace to our nation and world.

A powerful relationship with God does not happen overnight. Good, spiritual relationships develop over a course of many experiences. Our relationship with God is determined by how much we grow to love Him. The song "Oh How I Love Jesus," written by Fredrick Whitfield, says,

> *Oh how I love Jesus,*
> *Oh how I love Jesus,*
> *Oh how I love Jesus,*
> *Because He first loved me.*

Just think of how much He loves you and me. Loving Him should be a very easy thing for us to do. None of us deserve the kind of love that Jesus has for us. "While we were yet sinners, He died for us" (Romans 5:8).

He unselfishly gave His life so that we all might be saved. This love cannot be compared to any other. In Holy Scriptures, it is recorded that there is no greater love than the one who lays down His life to save another. This God-kind of love is the principle truth and fundamental foundation of the whole gospel. Our relationship with Him is just as powerful as our love for Him, for to know Him is to love Him. He loved us so much that He gave us new life through our born-again experience. To love Him as we should, we must experience the new birth.

Our new birth began with the repentance of our sins. Our belief that He rose and died again gives us the hope of our new birth. The biblical formula for salvation is found in Romans 10:9–10: "If you shalt confess with your mouth and believe with your heart that God has raised Jesus from the dead, you will be saved. For with the heart, man believeth unto righteousness and with the mouth, salvation is made through confession."

"If we confess our sins, He is faithful and just to forgive our sins and to cleanse us from all unrighteousness" (1 John 1:9).

Unfortunately, thousands of religious church-goers

have never had the true, born-again experience. Religion without the spiritual rebirth is vain. The Apostle Peter, after preaching the first sermon in the early church, gave the invitation to all who wanted to be saved. The Word says in Acts 2:38–39, "Repent every one of you in the name of Jesus Christ for the remission of sin, and you shall receive the gift of the Holy Ghost. For this promise is to you and to your children and to all that are afar off, even as many as the Lord shall call."

The precious gift of salvation and the Holy Ghost are available to everyone, because the gospel states, "Whosoever believes in Him shall not perish but have everlasting life" (John 3:16). After we repent of our sins, we can then grow in the grace and knowledge of our Lord Jesus Christ by faithfully attending a church where the full gospel is preached and demonstrated.

Yes, church attendance is imperative in spiritual growth. God's Word admonishes us that we should not forsake the assembling of ourselves one with another. David said in Psalm 122:1, "I was glad when they said unto me let us go into the house of the Lord. One thing have I desired of the Lord, and this one thing I seek after that I may dwell in the house of the Lord all the days of my life, to behold the beauty of the Lord, and to inquire in His temple." The gathering of God's people in church is a visible symbol of the unity of God and the body of Christ.

In spite of all of the negatives of the past, with God each of us has the opportunity to have a new beginning. "Come let us reason together said the Lord, though your sins be as scarlet, they shall be white as snow" (Isaiah 1:18). Our relationship with God should be free from the practice of sin because sin separates us from Him.

A good relationship with our sisters and brothers in Christ is also mandatory in growing in our relationship with God. My relationship with God started with a choice that God made before I was born. Jeremiah 1:5 says, "Before I formed you in the belly, I knew you." Before I called upon Him, He had already chosen me. As far back as I can remember I have had a passion and a longing to be close to God and to learn as much as possible about Him.

I can recall many times as a child, asking adults questions about God. One of the questions I remember asking, to which I already knew the answer, was, "Is it possible on earth to live a perfect and holy life?" This question was quite deep for an elementary-school boy to ask. I would always challenge the person who gave the wrong answer. I would answer my own question by saying, "God would not ask us to be holy if we could not do it." Even during my childhood, I believed in the gospel of perfectionism.

I remember reading the Scripture in the Bible that said, "Be holy as I am holy and be perfect as I am perfect."

Perfection and holiness are the characteristics and nature of God. We are regenerated and born again with this nature at the point of salvation. It is a daily and lifelong process. It accompanies a life of sanctification, which is subsequent to salvation. We can never do this by ourselves. It is a daily growing process.

The blood of Jesus and the power of His Spirit, along with His grace and mercy, grant us this new spiritual state of being. God expects us to strive each day to be more like Him. This should be our greatest passion and goal, despite our human limitations.

As Jesus was found in the temple at twelve years old, I, too, often found myself driven with a passion to be about my Father's business. Even as an adult, I constantly seek for higher heights and deeper depths in my relationship with God. I often pray, "Lord, save me the more. Lord, do a greater work in me and through me." I am always hungry and thirsty after more of His righteousness. Bishop Charles Price Jones wrote in his hymn, "Deeper, Deeper":

Deeper, deeper in the love of Jesus,
Daily let me go,
Higher, higher in the school of wisdom,
More of grace to know.
Oh deeper yet I pray,

JIMMIE R. HORTON

And higher every day,
And wiser blessed Lord,
In Thy Precious, Holy Word.

The best of life is experienced through our daily focus on the things of God. All of us inevitably need God. There is no substitute for that need. When God is not present in an individual's life, there is an enormous void that nothing else can fill. He or she will continuously be reminded that something is greatly missing. It makes good sense to choose the divine source that can meet the all-sufficient needs of our life. For it is in Him that all fullness dwells. Without His presence in our lives we would be helpless and hopeless, and our lives would be meaningless.

The needs and benefits of having a close relationship with God are inestimable and immeasurable. One of the greatest benefits of walking with God is having the fellowship with others who have made the same choice. My love for God and my love for God's people has blessed and enriched my life beyond measure. I am so thankful for my passion to love all people. When we love all people, we love God.

Our relationship with those who have a relationship with God yields countless joys and privileges. We, like those in the early church, are unified to edify and esteem our brothers and sisters as often as possible. We should be there for each other through troubles, trials, and tribulations in life. We should rejoice together, and if there be any sorrow, we should bear our sorrows together. Because of our compassion, we should be sensitive to one another's needs. Our desire to see each other excel should compel us to pray for one another.

Some of our greatest blessings are the blessings of encouragement that we receive from others. This unified desire to promote one another positively affects every blessed facet of our whole society. This enhances everyone's well-being, and the hope of our success becomes incredibly great.

When God is the center of our lives, we have direction and definition in our daily attitude about life. When we acknowledge His will for us, there is fulfillment just in knowing that He is always there with solutions and reassurance. "When we acknowledge Him in all of our ways, He is sure to guide and direct our daily paths" (Proverbs 3:6).

We all, regardless of how spiritually and naturally strong we are, have trials and troublesome experiences. For every situation we face, I am strongly convinced that God has a way of allowing it to work for our good. I believe that God can and will intervene for all of us, that we may conquer and become great witnesses of His awesome power. The traumatic tests we encounter in life leave us with testimonies to encourage others. I am certain that the closer I am to God, the better equipped I am to help others.

Our entire human race is suffering for the lack of more men and women who will unselfishly give of themselves to build a stronger society and world. Each time God blesses us, we are in more debt to be a blessing to others. Whether saint or sinner, the human blood in our veins should motivate us to be or become compassionate toward the entire human race.

17

Love Thy Neighbor

Love your neighbor as you love yourself.
Mark 12:31

Too often, we think of our neighbors as those who live close by in our neighborhood. However, the biblical term *neighbor* includes all humanity. To love everyone is the precious will of God. We have been commanded by God to love our neighbor as we love ourselves.

One of the greatest evils of our society is hate. God forbid that we hate anyone. We should love every individual as an integral part of ourselves. We cannot completely love ourselves if there is any hate within our heart for any other human being. The entire human race is interrelated, and our destinies are universally tied with each other.

All of the commandments of God are founded upon

the foundation of love. Jesus was asked by a certain lawyer, "What is the greatest commandment?" Jesus responded by admonishing him to love the Lord with all of his heart. We should love Him with all of our soul and with all of our strength. Jesus went on to say that the second of the two great commandments is like the first commandment: we should love everybody as we love ourselves (Mark 12:31). I am convinced that only a God-kind of love can do this.

Everywhere I go, it is just a part of me to love everyone, even strangers. One of my most pleasant experiences was when I took my wife to Alaska. We had the time of our lives on the Celebrity Cruise. We enjoyed the first-class service we received from our butler, culinary service, and the upscale, classy entertainment. We met and made many new friends we will always treasure.

However, the highlight of our trip was when we arrived in Ketchikan, Alaska. After touring the city, we saw a Full Gospel church and decided to attend the service. The atmosphere was that of a high and joyful celebration. We immediately felt a part and joined in with all of the other worshippers. The pastor came over to me and said, "You are a minister, aren't you?" I smiled and responded, "Yes." He asked me to come to the pulpit, where he gave me the microphone and asked me to give them words in my own way. With pleasure, I gave greetings of encouragement and exalted them to continue in their spirit of praise. Just as I was about to close, the pastor said, "Please continue to speak!" The congregation responded by saying, "Amen! Amen!" With that, I gave my sermonette, exalting the congregation to praise the Lord. It was one of the most enjoyable church services I've ever attended. Even to this day, our ties remain, and it is obvious that this electrifying service and the meeting of these dear ones was divine intervention. Our hearts, to this day, still bind closely in the fellowship of the joy of loving our neighbor, whether it is in Davenport, Iowa, or Ketchikan, Alaska.

We know that God is in control when we, in our limited human capacity, are able to be this inclusive in loving people. This kind of love is called agape love, which is defined in Romans 5:5. This love gives us hope because it is shed abroad from the heart of God, into our hearts by His Spirit.

Every human being was born with the need to love and be loved by others. We were innately given a natural ability to be compassionate for humankind. This love is called phileo, or brotherly love. Phileo without agape is incomplete. Human love without divine love is futile.

Loving people is easier for some of us than others; some people are more loveable than others. However, God has made it possible that we can all demonstrate obedience to His laws of love. If it were not possible,

God would not have commanded it of us. Even difficult people can be loved. They need love sometimes more than others. In my interaction with people in both the secular and religious communities, I have come to the conclusion that all people can be loved.

The best of us can be tempted to behave out of character. We should never stigmatize individuals unfairly. We should always perceive them as we would want them to perceive us. Even with children, I have observed that they will react to their perception of our expectations. When we give them favorable reinforcement, they respond favorably. When we respond to them negatively, they respond adversely. With this attitude, I have been successful in reversing unacceptable behavior in many students with low self-worth.

We have witnessed the amazing transformation of the lives of numerous parishioners who have overcome devastating disparities. Numerous individuals have been beaten down by verbal abuse from members of their own family. Some of these people were told they would never amount to anything, because of being compared to many who have lived lives of failure in their families. However, we have seen miraculous change happen almost like magic before our eyes. After hearing the good news of the gospel of love, their poor perception of themselves astoundingly changed.

The success of our ministry is based upon utilizing the Word of God as spiritual therapy to change all negative perceptions and circumstances in the lives of all who come to us with these needs. We are known far and near as the church of holistic healing. Jesus taught us to do unto others as we would have them do unto us (Matthew 7:12). It is imperative we demonstrate this to the secular and Christian community. I can recall many times when I was tempted to do just the opposite.

When I was a student at Jackson State University, I found a glass case that contained $150. The glass case had the name "Donna Antoine" written on it. I was tempted to use this money for Christmas shopping. However, I found myself going to Alexander Hall, the girl's dormitory, to see if I could find Donna Antoine. I told the receptionist I would like to talk to Donna. She came down, and I gave her the glass case containing the money. I will never forget the excitement and joy that was on her face. This was money that her parents had given to her to purchase her necessary supplies for school.

I experienced a special inner peace and joy knowing I had exercised my godly conscience of honesty, and the joy of my integrity outweighed anything that money could ever buy. I know that God has enormously rewarded me for this act of demonstrating my Christ-like compassion to this young lady.

When we sow love, we reap the overwhelming benefits of love. Jesus demonstrated this kind of love when He took all of our sins upon Himself. He loved us so much that He willingly submitted Himself to torture, abuse, and cruelty at the cross. As He was horrifically mistreated, He responded with love by saying, "Father, forgive them, for they know not what they do" (Luke 23:34). Our reward for loving others is always returned in a greater form than it was given out. We reap what we sow and many times, we reap more than we have sown.

I often refer to an analogy that was made by one of the deacons in our church concerning sowing and reaping. He said, "When we sow one grain of corn, we reap a stalk of corn, and on every stalk there are many ears, and on every ear there are many grains." Therefore, when we sow, our harvest time is greater than our seed time. When we unselfishly give love, we unselfishly receive benefits that are endless.

Our neighbors may be people of different races, different cultures, or different religious backgrounds. In order to love as we should, we must come out of our comfort zone and cross over the borders of our biases and personal preferences. Our neighbors may be individuals with whom we have nothing in common. It always seems easier to stay within our comfortable inner circle of friends, family, and acquaintances. It profits our whole society, however, when we reach out beyond our comfort zone to accommodate others. In doing so, our interaction with others will raise the level of our interpersonal relationships.

It is important that we realize the significance of generating positive relationship skills as early as possible in our home environments. Mom and Dad would often say, "Charity begins at home and then spreads abroad." Jesus said that He wants us to be witnesses that demonstrate the good news of His love, first at home, then Judea, Samaria, and the outermost parts of the world (Acts 1:8).

Loving our neighbor can be demonstrated in many ways. Love is an action word. Love is known by the fruit it bears. Every action we take should be a demonstration of love for all humanity.

Some of the greatest hate crimes have been perpetrated by family and familiar acquaintances. Hate crimes are often seen within the same race, the same community, and by those who share the same national origin. Within my own race, I have witnessed too much Black-on-Black crime. I have seen too many Black-on-Black drive-by shootings. Likewise, in the White race, there have been too many White-on-White acts of hate and crime. This is not an exception to other races. This must stop! This self-destruction is not limited to only the low socio-economic class, but it crosses cultural and social statuses.

Violence and bullying in our school systems and

across our nation is on the rise. I attribute much of this to the breakdown of strong, structured homes with solid discipline principles. One of the greatest forms of loving our neighbor is when we unite as a community for the common cause of love and peace. When every facet of our community comes together as one with a mission, we transform this disparity into hope.

When we all take ownership of every problem and positively deal with it, rather than blaming others, we are more effective in resolving the social and moral problems in all areas of our community. When we stop saying "them" and start saying "us," positive change will take place. When unity is demonstrated, our entire human environment is strengthened. We should take seriously the message of our nation's Constitution, which was designed for the people, of the people, and by the people.

I strongly believe that the laws of God were meant to be used also as models for the natural laws that should govern our nation and world. The laws of God are based upon His righteous Word. "The righteousness of God always exalts a nation, but sin has always and will always be a reproach to any nation or people" (Proverbs 14:34). Righteousness has consistently prospered us, and sin has consistently brought destruction to demean our well-being. This is very evident when we look at current events in our daily newspapers.

As a former educator, I had the privilege of knowing what it is to love children who were not my own. It was a joy to see these young people excel above the negative challenges and conflicts. Our careers should be chosen to match our passion to serve. I chose to teach children because children are some of the most beloved of God. Even Jesus referred to them as the kingdom of heaven and the most beloved of God.

I had the opportunity to work with many dedicated teachers who shared a like passion for their students. Many of these teachers went over and beyond their call of duty to supply less-fortunate students with necessities, such as food and clothing.

At Christmastime we supplied gifts for those who would have been without had it not been for our efforts to assist them. During the winter months, there were those who came without coats, mittens, and boots. We took it upon ourselves to see that these children were supplied with the necessary means to endure the cold winters. It is difficult for compassionate teachers to teach when they know that Johnnie did not have his breakfast. We were genuinely concerned and interested in their total welfare.

My older brothers and sisters often spoke of an outstanding teacher by the name of Mrs. Dawson, who made sandwiches every morning to feed her students who had not eaten breakfast before coming to school. She was an excellent teacher because she was aware of those natural human needs that could hinder the learning process when children were less fortunate.

I remember Dr. Jane Ellen McAllister, a professor at Jackson State University, who was so devoted and dedicated to her students that her whole life was centered on her mission to produce quality citizens. She was so unselfishly focused and committed to her students that many times, she would have to be reminded to pick up her paycheck in the office.

My childhood consisted of many individuals who played a major role in convincing me that most people have a soft spot in their heart to show compassion for others. I must also make mention of an old lady from Clifton Street, whom we called Granma. She baked teacakes for all of the kids in the neighborhood and would invite us over to watch her make lye soap in a big, boiling iron pot in her backyard. She was a sweet and caring lady, but she apparently struggled with superstitious beliefs. She often claimed that the devil was out to get her.

One day when we went by Granma's house, she was throwing her shoe up against the wall, so we asked, "What's the matter, Granma?" She said, "That devil is bothering me again, baby," and she continued to throw her shoe until she thought she made him stop. The big black pot she used for boiling to make lye soap was loaded with leftover cooking grease, lye, and other strange substances. When her lye soap was completed, she always shared her supply with other neighbors.

During my childhood, neighbors always supported each other in all the neighborhoods where I lived. I remember the Picture Man who would take our family pictures and accept whatever we offered to pay. I remember the blind man who sat on the corner and played his guitar. Although most of our neighbors had limited income, I still heard the jingles of nickels, dimes, and quarters that fell into his tin cup. With the sound of the jingling coins, I can still vividly hear him singing, "99½ Won't Do":

> *Lord I'm running,*
> *Trying to make a hundred,*
> *Ninety-nine and a half won't do.*
> *Lord I'm running,*
> *Trying to make a hundred,*
> *Ninety-nine and a half won't do.*

There was also Mrs. Emma Moses, who often sat me on her lap and gave me a slice of her homemade bread. Every time I saw her, I would say, "Mrs. Emma, loaf of bread, please?" This was my way of asking for a slice of bread.

All of those neighbors paint a collage of compassion and fond memories that I will always treasure. We thought Mr. Big Bill was wealthy because every time we asked for a nickel, he had a pocket full to give us. I remember Ms. Minnie, with all the fancy rings on her fingers, and Ms. Annabelle, who lived across the street in the two-story house—this was unusual for Blacks in those days. Mrs. Nancy and her husband, whom we called Mr. Good Man, always had a story to tell that made us kids chuckle.

I remember the corner store, Williams' Grocery. It was owned by a White couple, Mr. and Mrs. Williams. Our nickels and dimes went a long way; we got more than two cookies for a penny, and the Baby Ruth candy bars were huge. At Williams' Grocery, my sisters' favorite snacks were dill pickles and pork skins. We boys preferred the winding ball candy on a stick, ice cream, and soda pop.

There was a unified love among the neighbors. They could go next door for a cup of sugar, flour, and a couple of eggs to complete the preparation of a meal. These items were exchanged at different times by most of the neighbors, and no one felt embarrassed or humiliated. After moving to Davenport, Iowa, the image of the close-knit neighborhood went with me. I have unique and special memories of all the places I have lived.

The apartment at 930 Perry Street in Davenport was my first apartment. This was a neighborhood surrounded by Palmer Junior College, which gave it a college-town atmosphere. From there I moved to 1825 Winding Hill Road, where the neighbors were very friendly but less personable. It was in this apartment where the first Bible class took place. In June 1981, I moved to Sherwood Forrest, 1000 Blythewood Place, Apartment 117—the first apartment that Michelle and I shared. After living there for about three years, we bought our first home. It was in the basement of this home that Gospel Mission Temple was officially organized.

In all of these neighborhoods, our neighbors respected and admired us. My relationship with all of our neighbors was very genuine. They often called on me for counseling in times of trouble. I performed many of their marriage ceremonies and eulogized many of their family and friends. They often called upon me with their prayer requests.

In April 2004, we moved into our new spacious home. Although our new neighborhood consisted of more affluent and well-to-do neighbors, we were just as fond of the less affluent and less privileged neighbors from our old neighborhood.

Our new home was built to facilitate not only our immediate family but the vast number of family and friends who often visit throughout the year. Our home was built with six bedrooms and three levels of living space. I now enjoy the luxury that only the White middle class enjoyed when I was a boy in Mississippi. This home exceeds my highest dream. To God be the glory. We built this house to fulfill the attributes of the Word of God that encourages us to express our love to others through the spirit of hospitality.

I love people! I have a supernatural need to love all people. I am greatly fulfilled when people let me love them. Oftentimes, I am faced with the fact that some people are so insecure that they become very uncomfortable when people show them this great kind of unconditional love.

My love for people compels me to want the best for everybody. This kind of love is a godly love and seeks nothing in return. There are those who are easy to love because they are open to love and are loveable. On the other hand, there are those who want less for themselves than what God or I want for them. Our model of love is Jesus Christ. He came to this earth to show us how to love. Many times He came to people who refused to receive Him, even those He loved the most. But to those who will receive Him, He will give power to enjoy the benefits as His own dear children.

If we love like Christ has loved us, even the most difficult people will respond to our kindness and patience. We should never give up on loving anyone. We should love not only when it is convenient to do so, but also when it is difficult. Love even when you are dared to love. When we sow seeds of love, love returns in an even greater form. Love never loves in vain. Love should never have an ulterior motive. It never fails in accomplishing its mission of goodwill toward all mankind.

Let everything be done as if you were doing it unto the Lord Himself. Do it with a final-day-judgment motive. When I come into the judgment before the great throne of God, I want to make sure I have done my best in helping others to be their best. One day we must all stand before the judgment seat of Christ. We all must face the Great King at the right hand of God.

Jesus Himself told the story of the final and everlasting joys of our reward in heaven. He made this parable: "When we come into the judgment, we will either be at His right hand with the sheep or on His left hand with the goat. Then He will say to those of us on His right, 'Well done, thy good and faithful servant, you have been faithful over those things I have given you; enter into the joys of your Lord.' However, to those on his left, He will denounce to everlasting death and destruction" (Matthew 25:33).

We all can and should be philanthropists. Philanthropists are those who give a substantial amount of their resources back to society for the good cause of charity, love, and promoting the well-being of humanity.

This does not mean that we must have a wealth of money to accomplish this. These gifts to society can be simple, through our humble service of helping other individuals to excel.

The sacred mission of making a difference in the lives of others should be our motivation. This can be done with a consistent life of servitude. Sometimes you will not receive a thank-you or "I appreciate you," but your motivation should not be based on words, deeds, or expectant rewards alone. "Do not be weary in well doing, for you will reap the benefits you've sown" (Galatians 6:9).

When we love our fellow man, we are doing the work that Christ began while here on earth. He demonstrated His unusual compassion of caring to all whom He came in contact with. He was never biased or partial to anyone. Jesus demonstrated to us the importance of relating to those of low-estate so that they, by our influence, may excel to some of the highest levels of success in life. He specializes in transforming the "guttermost" to the "uttermost." Those whom He forgave most, He loved most. We will live better as we serve better. Each of us can do right, no matter our circumstances.

I am convinced that all of us have inborn tendencies to make supernatural changes in our community, in the nation, and in the world. I am encouraged by the words of wisdom of one of our special mothers of the church,

Mother Julia Howard. She has often said, "You cannot encourage someone without being encouraged, so if you want to be encouraged, get out and encourage somebody else."

Mother Julia was a very sainted mother who fervently demonstrated this kind of love in her life. Mother Julia once told me the story of how an impoverished man who lived in her neighborhood knocked on her door and asked, "Mother Julia, will you fix me some turkey and 'bressing'?" He had a speech impediment, but Mother Julia knew that he meant turkey and dressing. Mother Julia responded to this gentlemen by saying, "Of course, but I will need to go to the store first, and I will call you when it is ready." Mother Julia went to the store and shopped as if she were shopping for her own Thanksgiving dinner. She cooked this luscious turkey-and-dressing feast with all the trimmings and served this poor man, who became overwhelmed with joy because of her gracious act of love.

I am sure that those of us who would do likewise will one day, like Mother Julia, stand before the great white throne of God, and the Lord Himself will say, "When I was hungry, you fed me." When we ask the Lord, "When did we feed you?" He shall say, "My beloved, you fed me when you gave food to the hungry and that which you have done to the least among you, you have done even likewise unto me" (Matthew 25:35–40).

This kind of love is the supernatural demonstration of God's divine love. Naomi and Ruth in biblical times were examples of this amazing love. They expressed an exceptional bond that uniquely and profoundly reflected God's love through human vessels. The love of a mother-in-law for her daughter-in-law was exceptionally awesome. Ruth refused to leave Naomi, her mother-in-law. Naomi admonished Ruth to move on with her life after her husband died, saying, "I am too old to bear another son for you to wed" (Ruth 1:12). Ruth responded by saying, "Entreat me not to leave thee. Where you go, I will go, and where you lodge, I will lodge. Your people will be my people, and your God will be my God. Where you die I will die, and we will be buried together" (Ruth 1:16).

This love between Naomi and Ruth was taken to another level after Ruth married Boaz. She bore him a son and gave him to Naomi as a grandson who would be unto her what the Bible declared "a restorer of her life and a nurturer of her old age." She committed and vowed a covenant that she would love Naomi better than seven sons could ever love her. This love is similar to God's love: "Behold what manner of love that the father has bestowed upon all of us, that we should be called the sons and daughters of the Most High God" (John 3:1).

One of the most outstanding features of Gospel Mission Temple is that we are diverse in our racial, social, and economic approach to ministry. Our congregation is blessed to have Blacks, Whites, Hispanics, Asians, Puerto Ricans, and several other nationalities in our big church family.

The first to integrate our church family was a precious, White lady by the name of Beulah Gilbraith. She was mighty in intercessory prayer and praise. She was our first praise-and-worship leader at the Friendly House. I met her while teaching at Lincoln School. She was a janitor on the same floor as my classroom. Mother Beulah would always leave encouraging Scriptures on my desk after cleaning my room. She also became one of our most loyal financial supporters. She and our other church mother, Mother Mildred Spears, united together to form our first Mothers Board. Mother Beulah trained others in the congregation by leading the church in unified worship and praise. She passed the baton to a young evangelist named Tammy Trice.

Our love for all people has compelled us to reach out to the community, the nation, and the world, with over sixty ministries. We are so grateful that we have demonstrated to our children our active example of serving others with unselfish motives and attitudes.

Our daughter, Faith, is an excellent example of how a young woman can virtuously serve God through a committed life. She enjoys hard work and never complains about her role in the home, church, or workforce. Her greatest joys are the simple but profound things of life. She has always enjoyed serving others. Many times when growing up, we observed her doing chores that we assigned to her siblings.

Jimmie Jr. is also an excellent example of servitude. Even as a little boy, he often commented on how he admired the way I helped other people. While in elementary school, he wrote a paper that modeled his father and Dr. Martin Luther King Jr. as two of his favorite heroes. It is very apparent that Jimmie Jr., like our other two children, is blessed with a conscience that promotes him to uphold the ethics that were instilled in him from his childhood.

Avery has always been a people person. I remember when we took him and his siblings to the neighborhood park. Avery was about three years old, and Jimmie Jr. was eight years old. He and Jimmie Jr. walked over to a group of children, and Avery said, "My name is Abrey, and dis is my brudder, Dunior. What is your name?" This was the first observable indication of his gift to interact with people. All through school, he had a special way of befriending his classmates. It is very obvious that God has a very special calling on Avery's life, as he does Jimmie Jr. and Faith.

The teachers who taught me in the public schools

were more than schoolteachers. They were mentors, inspirers, confidants, and motivators. One of my most outstanding teachers, whom I remember most fondly, was my third-grade teacher, Mrs. Amnease T. Heard. She took a very special interest in me. I accredit much of my early childhood healthy self-esteem to her, because she often reinforced my belief that I was a very smart and brilliant boy. She invited me many times to her home and shared many interesting stories with me, which motivated me to strive for the best in life. I shall never forget how she invited me to her church, Mount Helen Baptist Church, to play the part of Herod the King in their annual Christmas program. I stayed in touch with her up until the time she went home to be with the Lord. Her daughter, Ann, and her husband, Jesse, are very dear friends of ours. Mrs. Heard left a great and memorable impact on my life.

One of the most notable icons of education that I must mention is Mrs. Ineva May Pitman. She played an enormous part in promoting education that has influenced generations of young people. Even to this day, she remains one of the great Movers and Shakers of the city of Jackson. She will always be honored for her lifelong contributions as a great social activist, educator, and religious leader.

My sixth-grade teacher, Mrs. LaPearl Wade Grant, was also an inspiration to me. She would always begin our school day at Isabel School with devotion that included a Scripture, a song, and a prayer. She would also talk to us about living our lives to obtain the best. She especially encouraged me to play the piano.

My first music teacher was Mrs. Josephine McKay. She was a very good teacher. She always taught with a baton in her hand, which she used to point to the music as her students played. I remember how she would strike the page when we struck the wrong note. She charged $2.50 for a month of eight lessons. She often told me I was one of her best students. She would sit out on the swing on her front porch and give me words of encouragement after my piano lessons.

I did not own a piano. Ms. Annie Terrell graciously allowed me to practice on her piano until I bought my own for fifteen dollars. It was an old Beckwith upright piano. She was an angel in disguise. During the earliest stages of my youth, I was encouraged by Ms. Annie and her sister, Ms. Onnie Terrell. These two sisters saw unusual potential in me and often inspired me to continue to set and attain high goals both spiritually and scholastically. During my first year of studying piano, Ms. Annie Terrell allowed me to practice every day on her piano. She remained one of those angels that nurtured me through her constant verbal motivation well into my adulthood. Today I treasure those precious memories.

As I advanced in music, Mr. Ross Clay taught me more professionally. He was a music perfectionist. Mr. Clay was also my professor of music education at Jackson State University. All of his students were very fond of him. He had a great sense of humor, and he often gave us motivational speeches.

Mr. Clay once told us that we should make the best of our time at Jackson State. He said, "Too many of you are standing out in front of the student union building, hugging and kissing, eating peanuts, lying, flunking out of class, and disappointing your mama and papa, who are picking cotton to send you to school." I remember a young lady once asked him how she did on a test. Mr. Clay, who often stammered, responded, "You ... you ... did ... did ... all right on the test, little gal, but you are ugly." The young lady broke out in laughter.

My sister Ann, who was a young widow, went back to college and took a music class from Mr. Clay. One day he came over to her desk and said, "What are you doing, sitting here with your legs crossed? These young men don't want you; you are a secondhand woman." My sister and all of the students who overheard him burst with laughter.

Mr. Clay lived to be over one hundred years old. While he was in his nineties, he called upon me to pray for him as he prepared to make sure that he would be ready when his time came to depart this life. He asked me to write a prayer that he could pray every day, so his soul would be well when his time came to depart. I am sure he is now with the Lord. I am grateful Mr. Clay knew the difference between going to church and what it is to be a real Christian. We must love our fellowmen so much that we want all of them to make peace with God through the salvation of their soul.

I will always love those who have inspired me. This includes more than my public school and college instructors; I am referring to people like my dear Sunday school teacher, Mrs. Ethel Dyson. She was very thorough in her knowledge of the entire Bible, but she always uniquely simplified it by teaching profound lessons through precepts and examples.

I must also mention Mrs. Agnes Nelson, our church organist, who gave me the first opportunity to play the piano for church service. I will never forget how special she made me feel when she learned I could play hymns. I was so highly honored that she allowed me to accompany her on the piano while she played the organ for Sunday morning services. She played only the hymns that I could play until I became an advanced church musician. I later became the official piano accompanist for both the junior and senior choir, thanks to the mentorship of Mrs. Nelson. She gave me the opportunity to express my God-given gift and love for ministering through music. I wrote a poetic tribute to her, titled "Ode to Mrs. Agnes Nelson." I was deeply moved when I saw this poem included on her home-going program.

Throughout my elementary, high school, and college days, some of my most treasured memories were my experiences with choral music. Most memorable is my participation in the Jackson State University Choir. I sang in the operas, *Aida* and *Turandot*, which were sponsored by Opera South. Another one of my enjoyable experiences was when I accompanied Reverend Ira Jefferson and Mrs. Anita Jefferson on a Sunday morning television show. It was like a Carnegie Hall experience.

Not only did they inspire me musically, but they contributed a wealth of support and Christian leadership to our entire youth department at Third Temple Church. I will always treasure our lifelong relationship as we continue to remain advocates for excellence in our pursuit of total Christian servitude to humanity.

Loving our neighbor includes encouraging our youth. This is exactly what these individuals did for me. I am so glad I took the time to tell them how much I loved and appreciated each of them.

18

Trust in God's Unlimited Ability

*Trust in the Lord with all of your heart
and lean not to your own understanding.*
Proverbs 3:5

God is trustworthy. He is almighty. He is unlimited in His ability, and He can do anything but fail. Even as a little boy, I can recall numerous times when I demonstrated unusual trust in Him. One of my favorite childhood songs expresses the foundation of my awesome trust in the almightiness of God. The song is entitled "God Can Do Anything but Fail" and written by Jesse Dixon:

> God can do anything, anything, anything,
> God can do anything but fail.
> He is Alpha and Omega,
> The beginning and the end.

He is the fairest of 10,000 to my soul.
God can do anything, anything, anything,
God can do anything but fail.

When we trust Him with all of our heart, we can be assured of His peace and security. Our trust in God gives us access to all that He is, all that He has, and all that He can do. Wholeheartedly trusting in Him equips us with the belief that there is nothing too hard for Him to perform. Even at our best, we are limited. It is important to realize that many of our problems are not resolved because we fail to totally rely on God's supernatural intervention.

At various times in our lives, we experience problems that may be overwhelming and complex. It is at these times we may not find any human place to turn for help and thereby need to rely solely on the master problem solver Himself. We should have the attitude of David when he said, "I will look unto the hills from which comes my help. My help comes from the Lord which made the heaven and earth" (Psalm 121:1, 2). God is the author and creator of all things. He has the all-sufficient knowledge and ability to reverse anything that may be opposed to our welfare.

One of the most trying times in my life was when my father was diagnosed with prostate cancer in his early eighties. It was devastating. The doctor's report was very bleak, but I immediately tapped into my spiritual storehouse of faith and began to recall the words my father taught me. This Word from Holy Scripture said, "Trust in the Lord with all of your heart and lean not to your own understanding. In all of your ways acknowledge Him and He will direct your path" (Proverbs 3:5-6). I immediately began to pray. I asked God to spare my father's life. I began to recall how faithful Dad had been in serving the Lord for many years. In spite of the doctor's diagnoses and prognosis, I utilized my faith. Miraculously, God heard my prayer. Dad lived to see his one hundredth year and was full of life and good health. This is a very good example of how our trust in God empowers the outcome of our prayers. This experience led me to share with my wife and children what I would like them to do if I ever faced a situation of that nature.

I reminded Jimmie Jr. of how I am confiding in him as my medical doctor; however, I made it clear to him that I am expecting him to utilize his faith and prayers for me as I did for my father. I told him that I am sure that he would be wise enough to use his medical expertise but ultimately confide in God and utilize his faith in God's miraculous healing power. Our help is in the name of the Lord.

Medical science is indeed a special gift from God,

but our greatest source of healing comes from the Great Physician Himself. Every good gift comes from the Lord, but our trust should not be focused on the gift. Our focus and trust should be on the giver. The quality of our lives would be absolutely nothing without God.

As a young married couple, Michelle and I learned to trust in God during trying times while parenting. When Jimmie Jr. was just a toddler, his legs were unusually bowed and fragile. We made several trips to the doctor but the condition only worsened. It was very devastating to see our little boy's legs literally bend as he would walk or while just standing. We did what we knew would always work; we confided in God for help. I remember that prayer verbatim: "Lord, please heal our little boy, and we will return it unto you with greater praise and thanksgiving." We did not wait until he was totally healed; rather, we praised God before the healing was totally manifested. After a short period of time, Jimmie Jr.'s legs were straight and strong. It was a miracle. I am sure that his healing took place at the moment of our belief. The *manifestation* of the healing took place shortly after.

It is imperative that we trust God not only in the time of need, but even when all is well. It is essential that we rely on Him to be our God, not only in sunshine and fair weather, but also in tempestuous times of trial and tribulation. It is important that we learn as much as we can in a personal way about the almightiness of God. We can only trust Him at the level of our confidence in Him. We should completely put our trust in Him because He is

Jehovah Rapha, The Lord that Heals Me;
Jehovah Nissi, The Lord, My Banner of Protection;
Jehovah Jireh, The Lord Will Provide;
Jehovah Shalom, The Lord, Our Peace;
Jehovah Misqabbi, The Lord, My High Tower;
Jehovah Tsidkenu, The Lord, Our Righteousness;
Jehovah M'gaddishcem, The Lord, Our Sanctifier;
Jehovah Bara, The Lord Creator;
Jehovah 'Ez-Lami, The Lord, My Strength; and
Jehovah Machsi, The Lord, My Refuge.

The psalmist David said, "The Lord is my Shepherd and I shall not want," and it is a universal favorite (Psalm 23:1). It gives us the blessed assurance that we can rely on the sufficiency of God's infinite ability to provide for all of our natural and spiritual needs. When we rely on our Shepherd to supply all we need, it is then that God positions Himself to bring His beloved sons and daughters total fulfillment.

Many times we experience lack because we do not utilize all of the resources that God has made available to us. As the disciple James wrote in his epistle, "We have not because we ask not. We ask and receive not because we ask with the wrong motive" (James 4:3). This is to say that we should trust in God enough to feel free to make our pleas known to Him. We should not, however, be selfish in petitioning our requests. He cares for us even more than the best of us could ever care for our children.

Jesus Himself reminds us that if our son asked for bread, we would not give him a stone; if he asked for a fish, we would not give him a serpent. If we would do our best to fulfill the needs of our children, we should consider how our Heavenly Father would do incomparably more for us.

Faith and trust are inseparable. We cannot have faith in God without trusting Him, and we cannot trust Him without using our faith in Him. Trust is the application of our faith. Our trust in God is a demonstration of our faith in His integrity and sovereignty.

God is who He says He is, and He can do absolutely everything He says He can do. He is the absolute essence of the assurance of His own Word. He does not need to swear by heaven or by earth; the solid evidence of His Word is all that we need to be absolute in our beliefs as we daily apply our undaunted faith in the unfailing almightiness of God.

19

The Christ-Centered Life

For me to live is Christ.
Philippians 1:21

Without Christ, life is meaningless. God gave us the best reflection of life when He gave Himself to us in human form through the Spirit of His Son, Jesus the Christ. His ultimate purpose was to deliver us from the jaws of death and give us the hope of eternal life through His precious blood.

When Jesus died for us, He saved us from death. Since He saved us from death, our decision to follow Him by living a committed Christian life should be the easiest decision we ever make. A "Christ-centered" life means just that. When we live with Christ as our chief focus, our lives are complete and totally fulfilled. A few years ago, there was a popular acronym, WWJD, which stood for "What Would Jesus Do?" When we ask and answer this question in our decision making, we can't go wrong.

Success without Christ is as morbid as a body without breath. God's unlimited success plan for your life will immediately begin the moment you accept Him as your Savior (Romans 9:9–10). When you ask the Lord Jesus Christ to come into your heart and believe that He is risen from the dead, He will forgive and cleanse you from all sin. As that very moment, you become an heir to all that God has and all that God is. Congratulations and welcome to the family of faith, and may you be overwhelmed with endless blessings and joy! After you have made that monumental decision, it is crucial that you find a church that ministers to your total well-being. The Bible says, "Forsake not the assembling of yourself together" (Hebrews 10:25). You need church, and church needs you.

Living a Christ-centered life does not mean we are superhuman, but it means we are guided by the supernatural power of God's presence. There is an old spiritual hymn, "Lord, I Want to Be a Christian," that symbolizes this truth:

> *Lord, I want to be a Christian,*
> *In my heart, in my heart,*
> *Lord, I want to be a Christian,*
> *In my heart.*

LIVE THE UNLIMITED LIFE

In order to live the Christ-centered life, we need supernatural help, because our human abilities are limited. It is imperative that we have the presence of Christ in our lives in order to live the Christian life. We can be like Christ when we give Him the liberty of having full control. The Christ-centered life is not only the better way of life, but it also is the best and only true way of life. Jesus Himself has declared, "He is the only way, He is the only truth, and He is The Life" (John 14:6).

Sometimes our pursuit in following the footsteps of Jesus may be tough. We may find ourselves experiencing the same types of trials, tribulations, and challenges as He did when He walked the earth. You are not a victim of defeat but through Him, "You are more than a conqueror and more than a winner" (Romans 8:37). Saints and sinners alike, will experience some form of suffering in life, but it is more profitable to suffer as a Christian than as a nonbeliever. Jesus has promised us, "If we suffer with Him, we will also reign with Him" (2 Timothy 2:12).

I am deeply concerned about these groups that claim to be Christians but who produce individuals that defy the very essence of who Jesus is. A Christian life should reflect the image that allows others to clearly see who Jesus is. Jesus, while teaching on the Mount of Olive, said, "You are the salt of the earth. You are the light of the world. Let your light so shine that others may see your good works and glorify your Father which is in heaven" (Matthew 5:13–16).

We are known by what others see us put into action. We speak louder by what we do than by what we say. We are true Christians when we show others how to live the Christ-like life. Jesus said, "People will know that you are my followers if you show them the kind of love that I have by loving one another" (John 13:35). Jesus is our source of life; therefore, when we follow in His footsteps, we cause others to believe that the Christian way is the best way of life.

Many times, we are not honest with ourselves and others when we deny the fact that although we are believers, we have our moments of discouragement and disappointments. When we are realistic with ourselves and others concerning our human challenges, we become more effective witnesses. We must be mindful of the sensitivity of those who have not yet been converted to the reality of knowing a true relationship with Christ.

It is imperative that every believer seek to be baptized in the life-giving Spirit of Jesus Christ. This Spirit is better known as the Holy Ghost and Spirit of Truth. We should not be ashamed or embarrassed to call this Spirit by the same name that Jesus did in Acts 1:5. He said, "John truly baptized you in water but you will soon be baptized with the Holy Ghost."

God wants us to be His witnesses so much that He gave us His Son, who gave His life by shedding His blood to wash us from all of our sins. He multiplied our spiritual benefits when He gave us the powerful presence of the Holy Ghost. The Holy Ghost is our indwelling power to demonstrate the characteristics of Jesus, the Truth and the Life.

When we make Jesus the center of our lives, we become very sensitive to forsaking all distractions that may hinder our spiritual focus on the things that pertain to pleasing Him. It is important that we love everybody, but we should not be influenced by everybody. We should be aware of the fact that we can be hindered by influences that are marching to the beat of another drummer.

Jesus prayed a special prayer for us just before He went back to His Father in heaven. He prayed, "Father, I pray not that you take them out of the world but keep them from the evils of the world" (John 17:15). It was His fervent prayer that we be "sanctified" or set apart from the evils of this world, that we may glorify God as Jesus did when He was on the earth. Jesus highly emphasized how we should not only be saved from the sin of the world but that we should also live a clean lifestyle.

The term "sanctified" has been misunderstood by many religious and nonreligious groups. Too many times, this term has been misinterpreted with negative stigmas that stereotype devout Christians as unpolished and ignorant. However, time has proven that people of holiness and sanctified persuasions make up a large population of society's highly intellectual, refined, and affluent individuals. Society is remarkably changing their vague misconception of this.

Jesus was a Nazarene. Nazareth was stigmatized as a town of common, low socio-economic citizens. He was despised and rejected by certain facets of society but did not retaliate. We should never let our pursuit of living a holy and a sanctified life cause us to turn people off with our overly zealous desire to impress.

A life of sanctification and holiness should be so appealing that we draw others to Christ. This is the kind of life that lifts Him up through our daily deeds and actions. When we do this, we fulfill the Scripture, "If I be lifted up, I will draw all men unto me" (John 12:32). When we draw all men to Christ, it is then that we know our sanctification and holiness is genuine. Too often, so-called "devout Christians" do a very poor job of showing the love, compassion, and sweet spirit of our loving Lord. When we commit ourselves to becoming real Christians, we follow His excellent example.

The pathway we walk in following Jesus is not always filled with a bed of roses. Yes, there are many roses, but there are also many thorns. Those of us who live for God must also experience adversities. "There are many afflictions for those who follow Christ, but He has promised to deliver us out of every one of them" (Psalm 34:19).

As Jesus encouraged His disciples while on earth, He assured them of the blessings of persecution when He said, "Blessed are you that are persecuted for the cause of doing what is right and following me. For great is your reward in heaven. For as you are persecuted now, so were the holy prophets that were before you" (Matthew 5:11, 12). When we make Jesus our chief focus, we must unselfishly follow Him. As we follow His path, we must first deny ourselves and then take up our cross as He guides our way.

It is important that we also deny the selfish desires of our flesh. They are promoted by ungodly passions that may tempt us to displease God. We can be assured that we do not have to yield to destructive and ungodly cravings. Rather, we can choose to be led by our healthy and productive desires. Those of us who allow ourselves to be led by God's spirit are perceived by God as His very own sons and daughters. When we live the Christ-centered life, we experience His absolute blessings and favor, and we can experience them every day.

20

The Abundant Blessings of Forgiveness

He whom the Son sets free is free indeed.
John 8:36

The value of God's forgiveness is endless. We all have had the need to be free from the bondage of guilt and condemnation. After He has forgiven us of all the wrongs we have committed, we become new creatures and free from all of our past sins. "There is no condemnation to those of us who are in Christ" (Romans 8:1). Too often, millions around the world live with the inferiority of a guilty conscience. "For all have sinned and come short of the glory of God" (Romans 3:23). Be assured that He has promised to cast all of our sins into the sea of forgetfulness, to remember them no more.

A guilty mind and conscience does not breed a healthy, happy life. Guilt robs us of our joy. "The joy of the Lord is our strength" (Nehemiah 8:10). Guilt causes mental, physical, spiritual, and emotional problems. God wants us to have the abundance of His forgiveness that we may enjoy overwhelming love, joy, and peace.

It is imperative that we teach children to know that God wants them to walk in the newness of life. As a classroom teacher, I witnessed many young people who lived daily with many guilt complexes. Their unhealthy guilt seriously hindered them from enjoying a healthy sense of confidence. The lack of good self-confidence greatly affects academic and social skills, as well as general success.

My great success as a teacher is due to my strong conviction that all children are uniquely special. I am convinced that parents and teachers must first use diverse and effective methods to consistently build up positive attitudes in the hearts and minds of children. This cannot be completely done without exposing them to the healing Word of God. God's Word is the ultimate source of holistic health and healing. This includes healing of the mind, body, soul, and spirit.

Sin is the root of all devastation and guilt. There is no power that can remove this devastation and condemnation but the blood of Jesus. The songwriter

Robert Lowery said it well when he wrote "Nothing But the Blood of Jesus":

> *What can wash away my sin?*
> *Nothing but the blood of Jesus.*
> *What can make me whole again?*
> *Nothing but the blood of Jesus.*
> *O' Precious is the flow,*
> *That makes me white as snow,*
> *No other fount' I know,*
> *Nothing but the blood of Jesus.*

The abundant life that Jesus offers is of such enormous magnitude that the whole man and woman must be freely available and completely submitted to Him who gives all things.

Forgiveness tremendously affects the whole person. It blesses the person who forgives and the person who is forgiven. Jesus said, as He taught His disciples to pray, "Forgive us for our trespasses as we forgive those who trespass against us" (Matthew 6:14). Unforgiveness can cause stress and health problems that can also negatively affect our mental, physical, and emotional health. Some of these health problems include high blood pressure, heart trouble, insomnia, or ulcers. This kind of stress may even slow down the natural ability of the immune system to fight diseases.

When we forgive, we release the stress that can cause these health problems. These problems can adversely affect our attention to maintain wholesome and healthy relationships with family and friends. We must rely upon God's Word to assure us good mental health. "Let this mind be in you which is also in Christ Jesus" (Philippians 2:5). In perfect peace, He will keep us whose minds are stayed on Him (Isaiah 26:3).

Forgiveness empowers our inner person to flow liberally in the perfect will of God's plan for our lives. We should follow the greatest example of forgiveness that Jesus set before us. The benefits are enormously great.

Holding grudges robs us of our freedom to enjoy the blessings of knowing the Christ-like gift of redemption. The power of condemnation is removed when we lift the burden of holding ourselves in the prisons of hostility and bitterness. It is imperative that we refuse to be influenced by negative people when going through trials and tribulation in life.

Forgiveness is a "heart thing." Our hearts are the source of inner forgiveness and being forgiven. Hard-hearted individuals find it difficult to give or receive forgiveness. It pleases God when we follow the example that Christ set before us after His crucifixion. Jesus prayed, "Father forgive them for they know not what they do" (Luke 23:34). Those of us that are strong should help those who are weak in this area. I have often said to others, "Who is wrong is not the most important factor in settling a dispute, but who is strong can be the greatest source of peacefully rectifying a dispute."

God expects more of us than He does of those who do not have the power of God in their lives. As the Bible clearly teaches us, "If our brother or sister is overtaken in a fault, those of us that are spiritual should help the individual by doing whatever we can to restore such a one in the spirit of meekness" (Galatians 6:1). We should be quick to forgive others because we never know when we may need to be forgiven again. The old folks use to say, "The chickens must come back home to roost." One of the greatest gifts God gave to the human race is His grace that granted us forgiveness. As He has so graciously forgiven us, let us likewise be blessed by the pleasure of forgiving one another.

21

Take Control of Your Fivefold Health

I wish above all things that you prosper and be healthy.
3 John 1:2

"God helps those who help themselves" is a saying I have heard all of my life, and I have found it to be a true statement. God gives all of us the potential to succeed in every aspect of our lives.

God wants every human being to be healthy—naturally, spiritually, mentally, emotionally, and financially. Jesus died to save us from the effects of all forms of diseases. He wants our physical bodies to be totally well.

While Jesus was on the earth, healing the sick was a key attribute of His ministry. I believe there is hope, through the miraculous power of God, even to those who may have physical challenges. The same Jesus who healed all manner of diseases while on earth is the same today and forever more. He was wounded for our transgressions and bruised for our iniquities and by His stripes, we are healed (Isaiah 53:5). However, we have a part to play in gaining and maintaining good health.

Do you know that your body is the temple of God? About twenty-five years ago, God strongly impressed upon me to take charge of my body by saying, "I beseech you that you present your body as a living sacrifice, holy, and acceptable unto me" (Romans 12:1). I interpreted this to include my whole being. I should eat healthily, exercise daily, and do all I can to be physically healthy.

It is very important that we nurture our spiritual man. We do not live by natural nutrition alone but by every word that comes from the mouth of God. This is why it is of utmost importance that we attend church often and have a personal daily devotion with Him. We should pray, worship, and praise God consistently. The benefits of prayer are enormous. Our greatest connection with God is spiritual. "God is a spirit and all that worship Him must worship Him in spirit and in truth" (John 4:24).

Another important part of our total being is our mind. "So a man or woman thinks, so are they" (Proverbs 23:7). A healthy mind is necessary for a healthy life. The Word of God admonishes us to be transformed from the destructive elements of the world by the renewing of our minds. Healthy habits are imperative to our physical, spiritual, and emotional well-being. The Word of God admonishes us to think of the things that are true, honest, just, pure, lovely, and of good report (Philippians 4:8).

At sixty-three years of age, I am as healthy as I was at twenty-three. I feel good, and I am often told how well I look. Much of this accompanies a very optimistic attitude toward life. I am thankful that I am in perfect health. I go to the doctor's office only once a year for my annual checkup. I have never been admitted to a hospital or experienced any form of serious illness. The only prescription medicine I have taken was an antibiotic following a dental procedure. God should get the glory and honor, even in our victorious health reports. I continue to amaze my physician with my good health, and my reply is, "Only God can grant good health."

Prayer is one of the chief sources of holistic health. The prayer of faith always heals and saves the sick. It is God's will that we become free from being emotionally ill. We cannot serve the Lord at our best when we are bound by unhealthy emotional problems. We have an important part to play in order to maintain holistic health. God is our source of good health. It is essential that we trust the ultimate source of good health every day of our lives.

Good financial management is healthy. Financial problems can greatly contribute to many other health problems. Millions of Americans are suffering from serious health issues due to financial stress. God forbid that we worry about anything. When we worry, we are not trusting God to supply all of our needs. As in other facets of our fivefold health, we must spend our money wisely!

Bad credit is a sign of poor financial management. It's amazing how many people with top-paying jobs are in financial trouble. Michelle and I learned early in our marriage that poor credit-card management is terrible. We took control over our finances and began to properly manage our spending. Our credit report has been a great blessing in the purchasing of thirty-five acres of land and the building of the church facility that exceeds ten million dollars. I am strongly convinced that we provoke God to continually overflow us with increase when we are good stewards and manage our increase wisely. When we take special measures to wisely utilize our blessings, we send a message of great gratitude to God.

22

God Has Great Plans for Your Success

I know My thoughts and concerns for your success.
Jeremiah 29:11

God created you with success in mind. You were not born to fail; you were born to win. God loves each of us greater than we could ever imagine. He has plans for your life that will bring you success and give Him glory.

It is of utmost importance to give special consideration to the plans that God has for your life. He will make His will known as you seek it daily. Proverbs 3:6 reads, "In all of your ways acknowledge Him and He will direct your path." We acknowledge Him when we pursue the godly lifestyle that He has laid out before us. The way of the Lord is the path that leads us to do the things that are right and that produce outcomes that are beneficial to everyone. When we live the godly life, we bring success not only to ourselves but to everyone with whom we are involved, whether family, friend, or fellowman.

God-given success is awesome. Success cannot be calculated only by natural achievement. "Man looks on the outward appearance but God looks on the heart" (1 Samuel 16:7). "As the heaven is higher than the earth, so are His thoughts higher than our thoughts" (Isaiah 55:9). Success in His eyes is more than materialistic or tangible gain. Real success breeds real joy and real peace. It gives true and solid substance to our life. God can transform a life of failure into a life of great accomplishments. This cannot happen without God's help. We may sow seeds of success but only God can give the increase.

I believe that when we consider God in all of our choices, it is impossible to fail. I have always believed that I was formed to be great in the sense of bringing joy to God and all of those who have invested in me and my future. I have always wanted to live so that others would see me in a very positive light, reflecting the better things and the best of life. I am so grateful that I took heed of my parents' daily admonition.

It is my fervent prayer that my children and my future generations continue to build upon the rich foundation of success that was so nobly laid by our forefathers and foremothers. We owe it to them and to ourselves to remain faithful to the great oracles of truth that will allow us to truly say, "Surely goodness and mercy shall follow me all the days of my life" (Psalm 23:6).

The road to success is not paved with anxiety. God forbid we live with daily doubt and fear. We shouldn't force ourselves to be successful, but we should freely do our part and God will always do His part. God is not playing hide-and-seek with us. He is ever present to help us through every trial and tribulation. He will supply all we can desire or ever need. I remember many times when God intervened for my family and me. Michelle and I often recall how God has rewarded our faithfulness. We cannot fail when we serve God with steadfast integrity.

The psalmist David said, "Serve the Lord with gladness" (Psalm 100:2). Success is all about service. We succeed when we give our best to the work of the Lord. My wife and I enjoy serving others, especially members of our church family. We have never neglected our family or the body of Christ. It gives us great joy as we recall how both of us have diligently worked to make the church the kind of church it is today. We are honored to be able to say that we worked hard to see that God's house was eloquently and magnificently built. It was after that when the Lord blessed us to build our own beautiful home. When we put God first, we always experience success.

I am strongly convinced that the best in life comes to those who are wise enough to be good to God. We have so often heard the slogan, "God is good," and the others chime in and say, "All the time." As God has been so kind and considerate of us, let us seek new ways that we may bless Him. He deserves better than what most of us do for Him. Too often, people take God's goodness for granted.

I enjoy doing those things that please God, and I do them with an unselfish passion. My fervent daily prayer is, "Lord, let me so love you and bring you more joy than I have ever given you before." I believe that as God has favored my forefathers and foremothers, so will He continue to favor all of my generations. God is saying to you, as He said to Joshua, "As I was with Moses, so shall I be with you. Be strong and very courageous, obey my Word, and I will make your way prosperous and you will have good success" (Joshua 1:7–8).

23

Unlimit Your Mental Boundaries

Be transformed by the renewing of your mind.
Romans 12:2

Never be held in bondage by your own mental enslavement. Be transformed by the renewing of your mind (Romans 12:2). Our greatest battlefield is the battlefield of the mind. When we fail to conquer the thoughts that deter us from optimistic thinking, we limit the prospect of our successful destiny. When we think we can, our attitude is affected by those positive thoughts.

Our mind can either limit us or promote us. Our mind determines whether we set high goals or barriers of limitations. I recall a quote that we used when I taught at Lincoln School: "A mind is a terrible thing to waste." It has been said that most people only use a small fraction of the capacity of their mental abilities. When we utilize our human and spiritual effort, we remove mental barriers that can cause stagnation of our success. Even after we have given our best, with God's help we can have more. We have access to the divine privileges of the supernatural mind of Christ.

God has blessed us with some degree of mental abilities, but when we move into the mind of the Spirit, we experience the blessings and favor that surpasses human logic or reason. God wants us to know and experience the full breadth, length, depth, and height of the benefits of His love toward us. Our human minds are too limited to comprehend the fullness of these privileges. By faith in God's unlimited access, we can experience blessings that are exceedingly and abundantly above all that we are able to ask or think (Ephesians 3:20). When we use the mind of Christ that is within us, we promote the process of living beyond our human resources.

When we experience life beyond our natural ability, we have hope that exceeds the limitations of our human logic and reason. I admire those in society who have attained high levels of academic and scholastic achievement and who have also accepted God's gift of wisdom. We should never neglect to pursue intellectual and educational advancement. I strongly believe that education is a necessity for our society and world today. Unfortunately, some of the intellectually astute leave no room for God's supernatural intervention. Knowledge without wisdom can frustrate God's process of bestowing the wealth of His blessings upon you; the Word of God refers to these people as forever learning but never coming to the knowledge of the truth.

Knowledge without God's wisdom is dangerous. A good example of spiritual ignorance is the story of Nicodemus, who was a ruler and affluent member of the Jewish Sanhedrin Council. This highly intelligent man asked the ridiculous question, "Can a man enter into his mother's womb a second time to be born again?" (John 3:4). Although intelligent, he did not understand the basic truths of things that are spiritual.

God wants us to believe that He can do anything but fail. This becomes a reality when we act on our strong faith. Our thoughts produce actions that are birthed in the mind. If we believe that God can do anything except fail, that is what we experience. The capacity of our thoughts can seriously affect the measure of our victory in life.

My parents often reminded my siblings and me that we can rise above all unfavorable circumstances and situations when we have faith and are optimistic. Positive thoughts will motivate us to develop positive attitudes that yield positive consequences. My family never thought of ourselves as being impoverished.

We knew our resources seemed limited, but we kept a wealthy attitude. I know now that the blessed attitude of our parents tremendously affected the thoughts of us children.

Now, in my adult years, I am reaping gigantic consequences of heeding the optimism of my childhood. Positive thoughts give hope to situations that may appear to be hopeless. I am convinced that the worst form of poverty is when an individual becomes victimized by impoverished thoughts. Refuse to live below your privilege. Desire the best of yourself and others. Unlimit your thought process, and give liberty to the possibilities of total victory and success.

In life, you will choose to be influenced either by positive or negative people. It is important to love everybody but not to be controlled by negative influences. Good people are sometimes tempted to be pessimistic. This is why it is important to surround yourself with positive people. Iron sharpens iron; therefore, people who surround themselves with productive people can gain advantage by their influence.

Choosing to live the best life is accompanied by high expectations for yourself and others. I often advise young men and women to be very particular about whom they choose to marry. In teaching Bible study one night, I said that a real woman is not easy to care for. She comes with great responsibility, and her price is far above rubies. I also made a similar statement about the husband—that a good husband is a big responsibility for a wife. The responsibilities, however, become a pleasure, because with love, marriage is not merely a duty or responsibility; it is a real joy and honor.

24

Let Excellence Be Your Goal

He who has begun a good work in you will perfect it.
Philippians 1:6

Why merely be good when you can be better? Why be better when you can be the best? Why settle for a C when you can have a B? And why be content with a B when you can have an A? It would profit us all if we were to seek to make our good better and our better best.

Excellence is a process. It is a daily pursuit. Although none of us have reached its full measure yet, we should all seek to obtain it. Paul said it best to the church of Philippi: "I do not think that I have arrived or accomplished my goal, but I am not focusing on the past; instead I am reaching forward to those things that are in my future as I press toward the mark of the prize of the high calling of God, which is in Christ Jesus" (Philippians 3:14). Let as many who seek to be perfect or excellent be like-minded.

God wants us to have His characteristics. For He Himself said, "Be ye holy as I am holy" (Leviticus 11:5). "Be perfect as I am perfect" (Matthew 5:48). I often remind Gospel Mission Temple that God would not require us to do anything that was not attainable. He is too righteous and too just to require us to reach for goals that are impossible. "With man, it is impossible, but with God, all things are possible" (Matthew 19:26). When God says to be holy and perfect, this is His way of encouraging us to strive to become more of a partaker of His blessed and divine nature. We cannot, in our own human efforts, reach such goals, but we can do all things through Christ, who is our strength. This is the mentality that we should instill in our children.

Jimmie Jr. has been academically conscientious since elementary school. As a senior in high school, he ultimately acquired a 4.0 grade point average, but he received a B in one of his writing classes. He was so adamant about maintaining academic excellence that he wanted to retake the class, but the teacher would not let him. We learned that another student, who was his friend and of a different race, was given the opportunity to retake the class. It became very obvious to me that this was an act of racial discrimination. I came to this conclusion after gathering concrete evidence, because those who impulsively accuse others of being racist are usually racist themselves.

I made a special visit to the principal's office and explained that I thought the school should encourage this kind of conscientious effort among all of their students. I went on to explain further that the teacher's decision had a racist undertone, because a student of another race was allowed to retake the class. The principal was just as disturbed as I was about this matter. I also expressed that in my twenty-five years of teaching in the school system, I was encouraged to motivate students to pursue this level of excellence. The principal agreed and granted my son's request. Jimmie Jr. retook the class and earned an A.

On his graduation day, as he came across the stage, I was filled with overwhelming gratitude when I heard his name called, followed by the words "academic excellence." He was the first African American to graduate from West High School with this academic status. I was happy that he was so honored, but I was saddened by the thought of his being the only African American graduate of academic excellence in the long history of the school. It was with this same drive that he continued at the University of Iowa School of Medicine. He graduated with top honors and has become a successful doctor. Likewise, when Avery and Faith received their college degrees, we were filled with just as much joy and gratitude. We encouraged all our children and others to strive to give excellent service to God with the same conscientiousness.

When we reach for the top, we are blessed to live each day with benefits of a new challenge. Life is never dull or boring when we allow ourselves to do our best, be our best, and seek to attain the best. It is not selfish to want the best things of life when our motives are to benefit others as we rise. The more we have, the more we have to give. We cannot give much when our goal is to have only enough for ourselves. However, whether we have little or much, we should give with an abundant, pure, and unselfish spirit. One day while talking with the renowned Dr. Maya Angelou on the phone, she reminded me that her grandmother so eloquently expressed this concept when she said, "When you get, give, and when you learn, teach."

The Bible talks about a widow who had only one mite, but she gave with a humble and bountiful spirit. Jesus said that she gave the most. God wants us thoroughly furnished. The best witnesses for God are those who are impressive to the world. The glory of God should shine through His people.

The word "glory" in Greek is *doxa*, which means all that God has and all that God is. This refers to the endless and infinite possessions and abilities of God. Who would not be impressed with a God who owns everything and is able to do anything except fail? God manifests all these attributes through us, His ambassadors.

God has chosen excellence for all of us, but we must make the personal choice to receive it. I want all that God has chosen for me. I would be very foolish to choose to live below my privilege. "Without a vision, we perish" (Proverbs 29:18). With a vision, we set goals to live life with purpose and progress. Excellence should affect every aspect of our lives. Seek excellence in your faith, and it will produce excellence in future blessings.

25

Enjoy Every Stage of Your Life

The joy of the Lord is your strength.
Nehemiah 8:10

Never wait until tomorrow to be happy. Choose to be happy today and tomorrow. Redeem the time, and maximize every moment.

Oftentimes, it is a human mind-set to procrastinate the joys of life. I have heard stories of those who think getting a spouse will reverse the gloom of their lives. Others say, "When I get rich [or when I retire, when I get a raise, when I grow up, when I get married, or when my children get grown], I am going to enjoy life." Never put off today for tomorrow. Today and every day for the rest of your life, choose to be happy. It is a choice. We all have something to be happy about and something to be sad about. We should accentuate the positives and refuse to focus on the negative side of life. Clouds and sunshine come into each of our lives. Choose to live on the sunny side.

I often reminisce with my siblings about the times when we were children, growing up at home. We enjoyed the simple life. I remember how special Christmas always was, yet we never owned a Christmas tree. Instead, we enjoyed decorating the windows with the traditional large, colorful Christmas bulbs, which more than compensated for the tree. We did not own a television until the Christmas of 1970. My brother Eddie and I bought a black-and-white television for our family when he returned from the army. I will never forget how happy we were, even before we owned the television. We spent more time communicating with each other than children who watch a lot of television today.

Each of us received a toy for Christmas. I remember the little red Radio Flyer wagon that Daddy brought home after work on Christmas Eve when I was about three years old. He did not play Santa. Mother tried to play Santa, but we only believed for a very short time.

We enjoyed Christmas tremendously. We always awoke on Christmas morning to the smell of turkey, cornbread dressing, and all sorts of cakes and pies. Momma kept her baked goods in a very large trunk. She made delicious potato pies. Her layered cakes were always tasty. The smell of Christmas included the aroma of coconut cake, pound cake, jelly cake, and chocolate cake. On Christmas, we were all given large delicious apples, oranges, and decorative Christmas candy. I always enjoyed the sweet, large raisins on stems. The sound of Christmas was always heard in the streets. Children were laughing, skating, riding bikes, and playing games cheerfully.

Most of all, Christmas was Christ-centered. The Christmas program at church was awesome. We all memorized rhyming speeches, and Mrs. Agnes Nelson taught us Christmas carols. As a teenager, I was often called upon to present the Christmas play. Sometimes I wrote my own plays. One that was most enjoyed was titled, *Tributes to the Christ Child*. The neighborhood was lit with cheer and best wishes. Christmas was the time we celebrated the birth of Christ with peace, joy, love, and goodwill to all. Those were some of the happiest memories of my childhood. I am fortunate to have been raised in a family that was very close. We were very rich in all the things that really mattered in life. The good times by far surpassed the hard or bad times we experienced.

I enjoyed the special days and holidays as Michelle and I were raising our children. Our children were a lot of fun, and they enjoyed the happy home life that God blessed us to have. I am thankful that we were able to give them many things that my parents were not able to give us. Most of all, I am glad that we, like our parents, gave our children the best of those things that mattered most. Children grow up so quickly. We enjoyed them then and still enjoy them tremendously today. In life, even with its trials and tribulations, we can learn to enjoy the silver lining behind every dark cloud.

The Apostle Paul said, "I have learned to abound and abase and in all things be thankful and content" (Philippians 4:12). Our happiness should be built upon the foundation of the joy of the Lord. With this kind of joy, you can be joyful in spite of your circumstances. As the prophet Habakkuk said, "Although the fig tree shall not blossom, and although there is no fruit on the vine, the olive tree shall fail, and the fields shall yield no meat, there shall not be any flock in the field, no herd in the stalls, yet will I rejoice in the Lord and in the joy of my salvation" (Habakkuk 3:17). I have often referred to this kind of joy as *holy joy*. Rejoice anyhow; praise God anyhow.

As life moves on, I enjoy living. I enjoy my wife and children now more than ever. I didn't know that being a senior citizen could be as sweet—and sometimes sweeter—than being a younger citizen. I have privileges now that I didn't have when I was younger. Most of my life has been centered on a very tight and demanding schedule. Since I am in full-time ministry, I now set my own pace. Only God and my wife affect how I set my daily schedule.

I enjoy doing what I want, when I want it, and how I want it done. I say these things unselfishly. I hear God saying that it is my time now; it's time to take care of my wife and invest in my family at another level. I have chosen this time to grant wisdom and blessings upon the church and my future generations.

One of the happiest days of our life was on December 28, 2010, when Jimmie Jr. informed us that his wife, Hannah, was expecting a little one. We were so elated. We immediately prayed that God would bless them to come back to Iowa so that we could be closer to them and our grandchild. On March 15, 2011, Jimmie Jr. accepted a medical residency in Des Moines, Iowa. This was a prayer answered and a dream come true. We are so blessed to live to see our dreams developing into reality. We praise God for all the enormous blessings He consistently bestows upon us.

In the fall of 2011, our first grandchild was born. She is a very special joy to Michelle and me. Avery and Faith love her immensely. She was given the beautiful name Eleanor Grace. We call her Ellie. She is a sweetheart—our bundle of joy. I had the privilege of shopping for her first wardrobe. I bought little Ellie one of every newborn garment in the store. I selected a different color in every style. I also bought her some newborn toys. My, did I indulge! Michelle spent many hours crocheting cute little baby clothes, hats, shoes, blankets, and anything else she could think of. Many say Ellie is already spoiled. Well, I think the correct term is that she is already *highly favored and blessed.*

One of our most joyous occasions was the beautiful dedication service of our precious little Eleanor Grace unto the Lord. It was an atmosphere of angelic celebration. Ellie's maternal grandparents, the Asburys, were there to celebrate with us. Her maternal grandfather, Monte Asbury, participated in performing the ceremony. Her grandmother, Laura Asbury, was also bubbling with great joy. Michelle and I, along with Ellie's aunt Faith and uncles, Avery and Lucas, were also highly elated. Ellie was dressed in her beautiful snow-white bonnet and gown. She behaved as if she knew we were making a fuss over her. She was so overwhelmed that tears trickled down her face. Hannah and Jimmie Jr. were just bursting with jubilant excitement and anticipation. Our whole church family was joyously glowing.

I want to make sure we support Jimmie Jr. and Hannah in their efforts to give their children the things in life that matter most. We want them to be highly favored and live the kind of life that is balanced with all the natural and spiritual things that can last throughout all their generations to come.

LIVE THE UNLIMITED LIFE

I want to be remembered as the kind of parent who unselfishly gave to the next generation a legacy of eternal love, hope, and joy to live the abundant and unlimited life. I want them, more than anything, to know Jesus personally. I want them to know His unmatchable and unlimited love. I want them to experience the fullness of knowing how much I love them. I want them to leave every generation better than they found it and to challenge their next generation to do better than the generations before them. I want them to love the Lord with all their hearts and love everybody as they love themselves.

26

Prayer Is a Powerful Privilege

*If you ask anything in My name, I will
do it. Pray without ceasing.*
John 14:14

Prayer is our access to all that God is and all of the endless things the He can do. "The effectual fervent prayer always avails much" (James 5:16). I am strongly convinced that prayer absolutely works.

I always begin my day with my bedside prayer and prayer in my prayer room. Michelle and I made sure that our new home was built to include a special prayer room. It is the most blessed room of our house.

Each day before I exercise and have breakfast, I lay prostrate and pray in my prayer room. In this special room, miracles are born and curses are reversed to blessings. I always begin my prayer with praise and the giving of my total being anew to God. I give a daily recommitment of my covenant with God. I often say, "Lord, let me love You more and more every day. Lord, let me bring You more joy in a new and special way. Lord, let my children and all my generations hereafter love You and bring You joy that is greater than words could ever express."

I am convinced that the head of every home should have a powerful prayer life. The head of every home should have access to supernatural power to protect, provide, and prosper the entire family. Without a powerful prayer life, this would be impossible. The husband and wife should pray together daily. Michelle and I pray together every day. We never go to bed without joining together in prayer. We have prayed with our children and for our children every day. It is a true saying that the family that prays together, stays together.

Prayer is more than telling God what you want Him to do. Prayer is listening to the inaudible voice of God. Prayer, for me, sometimes is just being quiet and still, as I enjoy the presence of God as He ministers to my whole being. If Jesus found it necessary to pray, so should we. Prayer for me is a spiritual addiction. David said, "As the deer pants after the waters, so doeth my heart for thee oh God" (Psalm 42:1).

The model prayer is a prayer that Jesus taught His

disciples to pray in Matthew 6:9–15. This prayer is a very unselfish prayer. Never are the selfish pronouns I, me, or my mentioned. However, the pronouns us and our are mentioned because they unselfishly include others.

> *Our Father, which art in heaven,*
> *Hallowed be thy Name.*
> *Thy Kingdom come.*
> *Thy will be done in earth,*
> *As it is in heaven.*
> *Give us this day our daily bread.*
> *And forgive us our trespasses,*
> *As we forgive those that trespass against us.*
> *And lead us not into temptation,*
> *But deliver us from evil.*
> *For thine is the kingdom,*
> *The power, and the glory,*
> *For ever and ever.*
> *Amen.*

We should pray inclusively. Remember those who are in leadership, such as the president, governor, mayor, teachers, preachers, mothers, fathers, our youth, and especially all of our senior citizens. All prayers are always answered. They may not be answered according to our request, but God sometimes silently says no, and sometimes his silence may mean "yes but not right now." We can be sure that whatever His answer is, it is for our good.

God does not have to prove that He is God by doing everything that we ask Him. "Yes" does not mean He has to do it when we want it and how we want it. Never forget that God always knows what is best for us. Everything He does is right. He is never wrong. He cannot and will not make a mistake. The old folks used to say, "He may not come when you want Him, but He is always right on time." Cleavant Derricks wrote the song, "Just a Little Talk with Jesus":

> Now let us have a little talk with Jesus,
> We'll tell Him all about our troubles.
> He will hear our faintest cry,
> And He will answer by and by.
> And when you feel a little prayer wheel turning,
> And you will know a little fire is burning,
> You will find a little talk with Jesus
> Makes it right.

When we pray, we should pray with the Spirit. We should personally request the things that pertain to pleasing God, desiring to serve Him and do His will. James said, "We have not because we ask not and ask and receive not because we ask amiss or with the wrong motive." We should not wait until we get into trouble or become in need before we pray. Our prayer should include more than what we want God to do for us. Our prayer should also be full of worship, praise, and thanksgiving for what He has already done and is doing. We must remember that we honor God even through our prayers of repentance. When we repent, we rise above the negative effects of piousness and pride.

God delights in hearing and answering our prayers. He is not avoiding us. He loves us so much that He has made Himself available twenty-four hours a day, seven days a week, and 365 days a year. He is not respective of any person. He loves everybody.

Our church is a powerful church because we are a praying church. While walking on a certain street in Jackson, Mississippi, the Lord spoke into my spirit: "My house shall be called the house of prayer." I was so deeply moved by this experience that I was led to return to Davenport and organize a seven-day-a-week intercessory prayer team. As soon as this went into effect, every department of the church escalated, as the whole church was empowered through our great faith in a God who is able to do all things. When we petition the throne of God, the heavens open and our infinite help comes from our God who is all-powerful, always present, and all-knowing. He remains the same, consistently without end.

27

Always Put God First

Seek ye first the kingdom of God and His righteousness.
Matthew 6:33

Our life's goal should be determined by what matters most. The things of God should be at the top of our priority list. I am certain that when we do this, we put ourselves in a position to align our lives with the blessed will of God. When we put God first and do our best to live up to His expectations, we experience the best of life's satisfaction and contentment. The Word of God admonishes us to "Seek ye first the kingdom of God and His righteousness and then the best of all things will follow thereafter" (Matthew 6:33).

God spoke to Moses and established the law of blessings based upon the following covenant: "Blessings are the result of putting God first." Moses then spoke to God's people and said, "If you will listen and obey God's Word, it allows you up to become recipients of His enormous blessings. God's blessings shall come after you and overtake you. He shall make you plenteous in goods, and God shall open His good treasure" (Deuteronomy 28:11–13).

I often think of my childhood memories of attending church. The Reverend Joe Ezra Bearden, one of the most sainted men I have ever known, was my first pastor. I admired and respected him immensely. Bearden constantly reminded the young people to set high goals for themselves. He would always add these words, "Put Christ first." This advice has followed me throughout my life. These words were echoed both at church and at home. I shall never forget a host of people who motivated and encouraged me.

I remember the old mothers of the church; they were so sweet. There was Mother Ada Jackson, who shouted every Sunday during the sermon. She was a blessing to know. Many times, she invited us to her home and gave us apples from her apple tree. I also vividly recall Mother Carter, who always conducted herself very formally and properly, especially when she spoke in church.

Then there was Sister Beulah Bearden, the wife of Pastor Joe Ezra Bearden. She always complimented me on my gift of playing the piano. She advised me to never let a church service lack for music when I had the ability to play.

I especially remember Mother Flossie Myers, a very feisty lady who was charismatic and full of spiritual fervor. She was very fond of me and often gave me the "Jesus first" admonition. She was a powerful prayer warrior who conducted prayer bands all over the city of Jackson. The impact of her prayers played an awesome part in the lives of many.

I will never forget Mother Sidney Austin, who brought candy to give all the little children after church. She was so sweet, and I loved to hear her pray. She would often say, "Lord, help us to lay aside *e-ver-y* weight and the sin and run this race with patience" (Hebrews 12:1).

I must mention Mrs. Beatrice Cooper, a "put God first" pioneer who conducted a children's Bible school in her home. Every summer she conducted Bible sessions with such excitement and enthusiasm that many children gave their hearts to Jesus. Mrs. Cooper would allow each child to say a little speech after the closing exercise on Sunday. At the end of the program, we were served homemade cake and ice cream.

There is no wisdom greater than the wisdom of putting God first in our lives. God endlessly honors and blesses those who live life with spiritual goals in mind. We should remember this, even in our finances. The prophet Malachi asked the question, "Will a man rob God?" He answered by saying, "Yes, we rob Him when we refuse to give our tithes and offerings" (Malachi 3:8). Our tithes are the first 10 percent of our financial increase. God has clearly said that we should bring the tithes and other offerings to his storehouse and obey Him. In doing so, He will open the windows of heaven and pour out blessings that there will not be enough room to receive them. He goes on to say that He will rebuke every entity that would intimidate His divine prosperity (Malachi 3:10–12). People of all nations will look upon you and call you blessed and a delightful example to all that behold God's favor upon you. This principle of sowing and reaping has blessed our congregation and our homes tremendously.

Your life will be as futile as gambling when there is no God-given direction. I am strongly convinced that God will add all of the needs and desires of our hearts when we give Him first priority. This cannot be done without a special love for God. This godly kind of love can be experienced by anybody and everybody who desires it. All who do not have it can seek it through fervent prayer from the heart. This kind of godly love is also an ongoing process of developing a close relationship with God.

I love the Lord now more than ever. I am so focused on Him that my life's greatest passion is to please Him. I personally know what the Apostle Paul meant when he said, "Nothing shall separate me from the love of God" (Romans 8:35).

Religious skeptics and critics do not understand the reality of an individual being so seriously involved with God to this degree. To them, we are thought of as overly zealous religious fanatics. Those who have never personally had this awesome experience will reconsider their opinion when they come to know God at this level for themselves. It remains very strange and almost foolish to them.

The wisdom of God is confusing to many who do not know Him but consider themselves wise. Paul admonished the church at Corinth and said, "The foolishness of God is wiser than men. God has chosen the foolish things of the world to confound the wise. These things are despised by those who do not understand wisdom in the sight of God" (1 Corinthians 1:27). He has chosen the simplicity of the gospel to amaze those who think of themselves as astute and wise.

We all were, at some time, a victim of making foolish decisions. However, God has reversed all of the mistakes of our past and has given us the opportunity to make wise decisions. As He has done that for us, His mercy and grace is sufficient for others. When we put God first, we have a passion to spread this good news to others of how it pays to serve Jesus. Frank Huston wrote the song, "It Pays to Serve Jesus":

> *It pays to serve Jesus;*
> *It pays every day,*
> *It pays every step of the way,*
> *Though the pathway to glory may sometimes be drear,*
> *You'll be happy each step of the way.*

Yes, sometimes putting God first may appear to be dreary, but you can indeed be happy each step of the way. God Himself will keep you encouraged as you daily experience His goodness and mercy.

28

Rejoice Even in Tough Times

God is our refuge and strength, a very present help in the time of trouble.
Psalm 46:1

Joy is a gift of the Spirit that is an absolute necessity in our daily lives. Without it, we would be emotionally unhealthy. When there is no joy, there is no strength. The times we now face in our nation and world are horrific. The moral decline is at its all-time low. The economy is at one of the lowest points in history. Unemployment has soared. These are some of the toughest of tough times, but I am convinced that with faith in God's promises, we can rejoice in spite of the terrible circumstances we may face. The joy of the Lord can supersede all of life's circumstances. Joy can dominate the spirit of sorrow.

I know what it is to have joy in the valley of despair.

Many times in my life, I have experienced the amazing blessing of learning to be content in all that God allows to happen. When my dad turned ninety-nine years old, I took the time to recollect and reminisce on the good and bad times.

I remember when times were so hard that Daddy was unable to pay all of the bills. He had to borrow money from a loan company and use our furniture as collateral. I remember his telling us how the loan company threatened to come and take our furniture. Most of the furniture was so old that they eventually reconsidered and let us keep it. In spite of the very fearful, gloomy situation, I remember the strength Dad and Mom showed through all of this. I never remember Mom or Dad laden with depression.

I remember my brother Eddie helping Daddy clean and shine shoes at the barbershop. While on his way to the barbershop, Eddie stopped to talk with the young men who worked at the body shop. That same day, the owner of the body shop accused Eddie of stealing guns from them. The police had a search warrant for our home but found no guns; the owner later admitted that someone else had taken them. In spite of the embarrassment of having the police come to our home, our home remained positive and optimistic. We were never taught to retaliate or render evil for evil. We were taught to love those who may spitefully use us. I am so happy that we were raised to be peacemakers. It takes a special strength to fight back with love and a nonviolent plan of social affirmative action.

Loving our enemy does not mean dealing passively with bigotry and injustice. My father was militantly against all forms of hate and human inequality. He often said, "When we are passive about any form of sin, we become participants and partakers of the sin and its consequences." We saw the community leaders demonstrate how to overcome evil with positive and successful activism.

In the midst of all of our sorrow, we had a hope and joy that surpasses understanding. I often say happiness can be affected by what is happening, but joy is what we have in spite of what is happening. Faith in the truth of God's Word is the only way we can experience this. David said, "I rejoice over the Word of God as one who has come into much riches" (Psalm 119:162). Another verse of "Negro National Anthem" is:

Stony the road we trod,
Bitter the chastening rod,
Felt in the days when hope unborn had died.
Yet with a steady beat,
Have not our weary feet,
Come to the place for which our fathers sighed?

Troubles and trials are also an opportunity to be strengthened and empowered with a greater faith.

Blessings are born out of trials and tribulations. I often talk with my mother about her awesome success as a wife, mother, home engineer, and doctor specializing in family practice, using her home remedies that always worked. We had little or no extra things. Most of our possessions were necessities, yet we were happy and content.

29

Respect and Be Respected

Do unto others as you would have them do unto you.
Luke 6:31

When we look up to others with respect, we honor God and ourselves. We always reap the seeds in life that we have sown. The old folks used to say, "What you send out will always come home." Respect and be respected. It is always wise to treat others with integrity and honor. A respectful attitude is contagious.

Our world needs more positive role models. As a classroom teacher, I set the tone to create an atmosphere that promoted and produced good relations, which became a part of each student's personal value and sentiment. This environment was highly advantageous to each child, the teachers, and to the whole school. I never tried to be a buddy. I learned early in my career that these young people needed and wanted teachers to be people that they could look up to.

When we witness to others by showing our Christlike ethical values through our positive people-skills, the benefits we experience are endless. I am certain that this can be done, even to those who do not show us proper respect.

On April 28, 1968, Dr. Martin Luther King Jr. was in Davenport, Iowa, to receive the Pacem in Terris Peace and Freedom Award. In his reception speech, he said, "Noncooperation with evil is as much a moral obligation as cooperation with good. So bomb our homes and threaten our children. We will still love you. Throw us in jail and, as difficult as it is, we will still love you. Send your hooded perpetrators of violence into our community at the midnight hour. Drag us out on some wayside road and beat us and leave us for dead. As difficult as it is, we will still love you. Hate is a tragic philosophy that ends up destroying the hater as well as the hated."

In this speech, Dr. King made it very clear that God is not just interested in our loving and respecting just the brown, black, or white people. He is interested in our treating everyone with love and respect. It is the right thing to do to treat the entire human race with justice and equality. Dr. King constantly reminded those who assisted him in his noble mission of equality that love and humanity are interrelated. These issues of human equality that affect some of us affect all of us.

When the message of respect is promoted and practiced within the family, workplace, and everywhere, all will greatly benefit. Our everyday lives are positively affected when people show respect one toward another. The principle of living with the best interest for others is healthy and profitable for everyone.

Our respect for our brothers and sisters is reflected through the way we talk and interrelate with one another, whether it is through direct or indirect interaction. The mayor of our city called to assure me that he was supportive of my activism for equality and social change in the Quad Cities. After a press conference held at our church, the mayor confirmed that our mission was accomplished and that he had allocated funds in the city budget to put an affirmative action officer in place. He reminded me that if he had more power, he would do more to promote the city's progress in all areas of our concern.

This kind of respect cannot be legislated in Congress; it must be implemented and demonstrated in our hearts. Respect is born out of our passion of love, peace, and goodwill to God and all mankind. Each and every human being must first respect himself. Self-respect is contagious. When this is done, we can respect others properly.

All human beings are endowed with the ability to believe and think positively about themselves and others. We were created by a loving God. We were created in His image. Each of us is given a measure of faith to believe that we can do all things; and according to our faith, so be it unto us. We have the natural nature that the Bible describes as "a little lower than the angels" (Psalm 8:5). Although we were all born in sin, we have power in our human nature to confess and possess the ability to do unto others as we would have them do unto us.

30

Be Blessed by Humility

He that humbleth himself shall be exalted.
Luke 18:14

Humility is wealth. Humility compels us to refrain from thinking more highly of ourselves than we ought. It keeps our spirits and attitudes in perspective. It does not diminish our healthy self-esteem or self-worth; instead, it merely keeps us from the horrific damage of pride and arrogance. It allows us, at all times, to graciously be mindful of the importance of preferring others, rather than selfishly focusing on ourselves.

Jesus was and is the most perfect example of humility. He consented to God's plan of suffering even unto death, which gave Him the divine title of the "Suffering Servant." He went down to the lowest chamber of hell so that we may become partakers of the riches of heaven and eternal life.

Humility is a spiritual thing. It is our nature to be human, but our human flesh cannot please God alone. We need to follow the example that Jesus set before us. He did not yield to His flesh. He gave up the will of His flesh, fulfilling the Scripture in Romans 8:1: "There is no longer any condemnation to those who diligently serve Jesus Christ and no longer seek to only please themselves, but seek to please Jesus Christ through everyday living."

Humility also blesses us in our human relationships. I have found that marriage is at its best when couples are free from selfishness. It has become a joy to consider my wife and those things that pertain to her well-being and her happiness. She, likewise, has made me feel that my happiness and well-being are her highest priority. This attitude and spirit can positively influence the lifestyle of our children from generation to generation. It creates strong security ties between family members. It will compel individuals to be compassionate, not only to other family members but to every human being.

God hates a proud look. This must not be confused with the good attitude of individuals who have healthy confidence and are secure. Their faith makes them feel optimistic about God, people, and all that pertains to life. They also have a positive attitude toward the hope of all of God's promises. This kind of faith breeds confidence and allows us to be optimistic in bleak situations or circumstances.

Pride is a form of insecurity. Humility has no need to be puffed up because it demonstrates confidence in the affirmation and blessed assurance of God's most reliable Word. My humble beginnings and upbringing helped me to keep my feet on the ground and walk very circumspectly of my noble mission to remain free from the evil presence of the spirit of pride. The Bible clearly states, "Pride goes before destruction" (Proverbs 16:18).

I often pray that I will always be a living example of the childlike humility that Jesus taught in the Gospels. The disciple once came to Him and asked, "Who is the greatest in the kingdom of heaven?" Jesus took a little child and placed him in the midst of them and said, "Except you become as humble as a little child, you will not be able to enter into the Kingdom of Heaven" (Matthew 18:1–3).

When our lives are guided by the spirit of humility, it is very easy to forgive others and not be controlled by the spirit of revenge when we have been wronged by them. God expects us to follow peace with everyone. When others offend us, we should forgive and be at peace for the benefit of ourselves and them. If we do not forgive, we ourselves will not be forgiven.

Humility blesses every area of our lives because it compels us to be completely subject to the perfect will of God. When we are subject to His will, we become recipients of God's total plan of favor and endless benefits. Without a humble spirit, it is impossible to please God. The pride of pleasing oneself, rather than God, is detrimental to our total being.

God's plan is the best plan. I am convinced that every human being is highly significant to God. Every individual's destiny was preordained by God. The wisdom of God's Word teaches us to choose the benefits that are the result of our complying with the oracles of God. Complying with these holy oracles is a sure guarantee that our best will progressively mature and dominate our lives.

Saul, who was God's chosen vessel, is a classic example of the terrible consequences of disobedience. He was denounced from the throne as king over Israel and ended up falling upon his own sword in death. Saul was never forgiven for his selfish and disobedient acts of rebellion toward God's holy admonition.

God is and always has been a God of restitution and forgiveness. His desire and passion to bless us is amazingly powerful. Humility is God's special gift of love that tempers our destiny of joy, peace, and total fulfillment.

31

Accept What God Allows

*All things work together for the good
of those who love the Lord.*
Romans 8:28

God knows what He is doing. He is who He says He is. He can do everything that He says He can do. "He is not like man; He cannot lie. If He said it, will He not do it?" (Numbers 23:19). It has become a part of my natural and spiritual nature to relax and rest in the comfort of my inner assurance. Everything that happens to me will work out for my good because God is watching out for me. Even in the time of conflict, because of Christ, I win.

Sometimes, even those of us who consider ourselves devout and committed Christians battle with spirits that try to attack us with doubt, fear, and insecurity. Many times when we feel that life's troubles unjustly befall us,

Satan himself will try to make his visitation and cause us to feel abandoned by God and to feel hopeless. During these times, we can conquer this by following Jesus' example after Satan tempted Him in the wilderness. Jesus spoke the Word and said, "It is written, thou shall not tempt the Lord thy God" (Matthew 4:7). When Satan departed, an angel came and ministered to Jesus.

As I look back over my life, it is very obvious to me that God has been in control, because both the good and bad circumstances have worked out for my good. It is apparent that God wants the best for me and is able to steer every event of my life in the direction that allows me to experience the fullest of my purpose and goodwill.

From my childhood and even to this day, God has proven to be my Great Physician. My parents knew nothing about health insurance. I remember how my mother treated our colds, flu, toothaches, and other small ailments, like headaches. She would grease our chest with cow tallow (beef oil) to rid us of flu and cold symptoms. Mother showed us how to make do with what we had and be thankful. We never went to a doctor. There were twelve children in our house, and none of us was ever seriously ill. This was indeed a miracle.

Raising all of us was more difficult than we will ever know. I believe if Mom and Dad had the choice, however, they would to do it all over again. My siblings and I appreciate our parents more than words can ever express. I often sit and think of better ways that I can be a blessing to them. It was such a blessing for me to see my parents' joy when I renovated their home. Although I have not lived at home for over forty years, I have never failed to see that all of their needs are met. Michelle and I always include Mom and Dad in our financial distributions.

Problems in life are so much easier to bear when we believe that everything works together for the good for those who love the Lord. As many times as I have heard this Scripture quoted, it seems most of the time the emphasis is placed on "everything works out for the good." However, not enough emphasis is placed on the second phrase that says "to them that love the Lord." This Scripture is referring to the endless and blessed benefits that come to those who truly love God. This wonderful favor is the result of our having a godly relationship—choosing to live the kind of lifestyle that reverences Him through the obedience of His Word.

Jesus said, "If you love me, keep my commandments" (John 14:15). Jesus once asked the question, "How can you say that you love me and not do the things that I command you to do?" (Luke 6:46). Love is an action word. Love is as love does. If we love Him, we should serve Him in action, word, and deed.

Love does not seek to receive, but it takes pleasure

in giving. In all of my relationships, whether divine or human, I have witnessed that God does all things well. He specializes in taking bad situations and circumstances and transforming them into victories and triumphs. Troubles and trials are blessings in disguise, and three young sisters—Shameka, Tanika, and Cherita McNeal—in our congregation are a very good example of this. The storms in their lives seemed endless and unbearable. Their mother and father were incarcerated, and they were tossed about into seventeen foster homes, in which they had some horrible experiences. However, they ultimately were taken into the care of members of our congregation, the Saddler and Green families. These families, along with our congregation, gave them the special God kind of love that miraculously transformed their lives. They blossomed into a success story super-extraordinary. Lady Michelle and I put forth special effort to give them personal, loving care. The gospel of the good news of the love of Jesus was offered to them, and they liberally received it. They are now testimonies to God's amazing transformational power.

    Michelle and I were honored in a special appreciation service; one of the most moving features of that service was when the McNeal sisters, who recently graduated from college with honors, presented us with a plaque that read:

> *To Our Dearest*
> *Bishop,*
> *You looked at us and saw*
> *our potential when no one else did.*
> *You were truly a beam of hope*
> *in our time of hopelessness.*
> *That was eight years ago.*
> *TODAY, we love you more*
> *than yesterday and only half as much*
> *as we will tomorrow.*
>
> *Thank You,*
> *Shamika, Tanika, & Cherita*
> *June 4, 2010*

After their reading this, there was not a dry eye among the congregation. To God be the glory!

The storms of life are opportunities to experience God's power. It protects us, even during the most trying and hardest times in our lives. I have learned that tribulations can be divine diamonds in the rough. They are checks that we can take to the bank and cash. I often refer to Job, the classical Old Testament patriarch, who said, in the midst of his dire and terrible encounters with a domino effect of hard troubles and trials, "Though He slay me, yet will I trust Him" (Job 13:15).

We can rejoice in the blessed assurance that God has a victory plan for every adversity that each of us who love Him may face. Just that truth alone should encourage us to not become weary or discouraged but to continue believing that He will give us what we need. It is important that we wait on the Lord and remember that through adversity, as long as we please God in our everyday lives, He will come through for us. "Be not weary in well doing for we will reap, if we faint not" (Galatians 6:9).

32

Be Thankful Every Day

In all things give thanks.
1 Thessalonians 5:18

It is important that we realize that everyone has a reason to be thankful every day. Regardless of how terrible our situations are, they could be much worse. There is an old proverb that says, "I complained that I had no shoes until I saw a man who had no feet." God's Word reads, "In all things, give thanks" (1 Thessalonians 5:18). It does not say, "*For* all things, give thanks." I know what it is to be grateful to God in unfavorable circumstances. To be thankful is to be appreciative to another for his or her acts of kindness. God has favored all of us in some way. Those things in life we take for granted are the basic things of life.

Too often, many of us take for granted our God-given

blessings, such as the use of our five senses. It is because of God's goodness and mercy that we live, move, and have our being. Sometimes we are so focused on bigger and better things that we lose out on enjoying the blessings of the basic things in life.

As I have grown older, I have grown wiser in my daily appreciation to God and to others who have in some way shown me favor. I have grown to be thankful, not only for His favor toward me but also for the favor of others, especially my family and friends.

We must come to the realization that God does not owe us anything. Everything He does, He does because of His awesome love for us. His love does not exclude anyone. He does not send the rains of heaven only upon the just but also upon the unjust. Because of his mercy, we do not always receive the consequences of our unwise decisions.

Thankfulness is more than mere words that come from our lips. Thankfulness is the expressed action that comes from our heart, which expresses our heartfelt appreciation. David said, "I will bless the Lord at all times" (Psalm 34:1). He did not say, "I will bless Him when He does everything for me when I want Him to, how I want Him to, and the way I want Him to do it." David was a man after God's own heart. He was not just after what God could do for Him.

We should be truly thankful to God and others for more than the benefits that we can get from them. We should be grateful for our family members, even when we are not happy with everything they may be doing. Good parents love their children and are always thankful for them. At times, we may disapprove of their behavior, but we never stop loving them.

Even after God had repented or was sorry that He made man, He reconsidered and continued to love us unconditionally. Thankfulness comes from our lips, our hearts, and our spirits. David said, "I will bless the Lord oh my soul and all that is within me" (Psalm 103:1). I will be thankful with all of my natural and spiritual self.

There are many ways that we can and should demonstrate our gratefulness to God. When we take measures to be good stewards over all the things with which He has blessed or entrusted us, we should show our appreciation through our action. For instance, when we do our part in making healthy decisions to take good care of our bodies, it is a reflection that we are not taking our physical well-being for granted. Yes, God helps those who help themselves.

We should have a strong desire to show Him how we do not take His grace, mercy, or love for granted. Even in our family matters, we should be very scrupulous and meticulous. When we show our thankfulness, God will bless us even more. We should never make our loved ones and friends feel that their acts of love have gone unnoticed. A simple thank-you can go a long way—say it more often.

I was taught the virtue and rewards of saying "please" and "thank you," even as a child. Those who hear it will be encouraged to oblige. We should not do this for selfish reasons but because it is the right thing to do.

I learned early in my marriage that a grateful attitude ignites the spark and flame in our love relationship. Even now, I do not take for granted my wife's delicious meals, the clean house, or her acts of kindness. Many times I show my thanks with flowers or some other kind of deed. I often buy my wife flowers just because I love her and not because of what she does.

This principle also applies to my family, friends, and all with whom I may come in contact. Our congregation is amazingly sweet to Michelle and me. They always show such enormous love toward us and our family. We consistently thank them and show them that we love and appreciate them. They make us feel like a king and queen. Their exceptional love for us is royal.

We have the finest congregation in the world! Loyalty and love always are compensated with loyal rewards and gifts of love. This love is divine and unconditional. Remember to practice thankful habits every day. Believe me—the more you give, the more you will have a reason to be thankful.

33

The Enormous Power of Praise

God inhabits the praises of His people.
Psalm 22:3

The act of giving God praise works wonders! This can be done through our words and deeds. Praising and serving the Lord is my greatest passion. We should take very seriously the great biblical proclamation, "Let everything that has breath, praise the Lord" (Psalm 150:6). We all owe God praise. We were made to praise Him in every facet of our lives. There is a praise that is referred to as the "fruit of our lips," but the greatest praise is the fruit of our life and lifestyles. God is more than worthy of all of our praises. I am strongly convinced that I was especially chosen and anointed to praise the Lord in a super-extraordinary way. Every sermon that I have preached has focused in some way on the power of praise.

My first sermon included one of the greatest praise stories, telling how the tribe of Judah won the great battle against the children of Ammon, Moab, and Mount Seir. The small army of Judah (praise) won the victory over all three armies that rose up against them, due to using praise as a weapon. This miracle happened because they had been taught by their leader, Jehoshaphat, the power of praising the Lord.

Praise provokes God's presence. The more praise we give, the more of His presence we receive. God will reside where His praises are. He inhabits all of the praise that His people render unto Him. Our church, Gospel Mission Temple, is very militant and passionate about serving and praising God. It is one of our greatest joys. We love the Lord so much that praise is just something that we do without putting forth a lot of effort. When praises go up, blessings come down.

Praising God should be an expression of the spirit, heart, soul, and body. We often say, "I will bless the Lord oh my soul and all that is within me" (Psalm 103:1). All that is within me is inclusive of all of my total being, including my emotions. God deserves our total praise, which includes praising Him by living the lifestyle that brings Him glory and honor. Each of us has many reasons to praise Him. The song "When I Think of the Goodness of Jesus" was written by Bertha James:

LIVE THE UNLIMITED LIFE

When I think of the goodness of Jesus,
And all He has done for me,
My soul cries out Hallelujah,
I thank God for saving me.

When we count our blessings, we can see how the good circumstances by far exceed the bad circumstances in our lives. We should praise Him for the past, present, and future triumphs and blessings. The psalmist David used his power of praising the Lord to encourage himself and also as ammunition to slay the giant Goliath. As the giant come out to attack, David declared, "The same God that delivered me out of the paws of the bear and the jaws of the lion will also deliver me from you" (1 Samuel 17:37). As it was spoken, so did it come to pass.

I am convinced that God's highest favor is provoked by His love and our allegiance to Him. Actions always speak louder than words! God loves us infinitely and unconditionally and we should demonstrate our love for Him through our actions. We show this kind of love when we live the kind of lifestyle that brings glory, honor, and praise to Him. It is very important to God that we prove ourselves true to Him through our commitment to Him.

When we fail to obey and honor Him with our allegiance to Him, we hinder the blessings of completing the flow of His divine favor. Our praise reflects our love for Him. He has clearly made it known in His Word that if we love Him, we will keep His Word. All of this is a living testimony to our true relationship with Him.

God loves His people, but His love and grace does not exclude His judgment. The prophet Amos warned Israel with these words: "Hate evil and do good that He may be gracious unto you. Because of your sins, God will not receive your offering or the noise of your songs. But let judgment run down as water and righteousness as a mighty stream" (Amos 5:15). We should, at all times, seek to do those things that promote His favor, rather than those things that provoke disapproval. This is the perfect will of God for all of His people.

The power of our praise is empowered by the way we honor Him with our lives through our commitment and dedication. When we put our praise in action, we are certain to experience the life of total victory and unusual favor from above.

34

The Endless Value of Wisdom

*If any of you lack wisdom, let him ask of
God, who will freely give it to you.*
James 1:5

Wisdom is the principal thing. Wisdom is greater than the value of gold, silver, or precious stones. It is available to everyone. God is the only true source of wisdom. In the book of James, it reads, "Whoever desires wisdom should ask of God, who will freely give to them" (James 1:5). Without it, we would all be helpless and hopeless. The consequences of making wise choices are great, but the consequences of making foolish choices can be horrific and may seem endless. The best choices can be found in the good news, which is the gospel of Jesus Christ.

An amazing Bible story in the book of Matthew is

the analogy of the wise and the foolish man. The story tells that the wise man built his house upon a rock that stood firm when the storms came. However, the foolish man built his house upon the sand. When the storms and winds came, the foolish man's house fell. The moral of the story is powerfully filled with truth and admonition. When we live the life of obedience to the Word, the storms of life cannot destroy or deter us from our blessed and rich destiny in Christ.

Wisdom manifests itself in many forms. It will shine like the noonday sun. It will yield the fruits of joy and not sorrow. Solomon, who was distinctly honored with the title, the "wisest man who ever lived," offers a wealth of wisdom in the book of Proverbs. Solomon was so wise that the Queen of Sheba and many others came to him to learn from his great words of wisdom and see the wealth that he possessed. One of the greatest lessons we should learn from his life is that wisdom should not be temporarily, but eternally, embraced and cherished forever. Never forsake wisdom, and it will never forsake or deceive you.

Wise choices can be generationally consistent and endure throughout countless generations. This, too, is the will of God for all families on earth. Your choices affect more than you alone. The wise choices that you make today can affect generations to come, just as the terrible effects of foolish choices can affect future generations. Your choices affect even those who have no biological connection to you. Even in social and economic aspects of society, we are taxed to pay the expense of those who have made bad choices.

There are many people in our society who are recipients of government welfare. Fortunately, not all government welfare recipients are abusing it, but there is no such thing as a free lunch; somebody is paying for it.

As by the first man, Adam, we all were born in sin, but thanks be to God for the second man, Jesus Christ. Because of His choice of righteousness, we can be born again to live a life of success and enjoy the best of the good life. We all, at some time in our lives, have made some bad choices. John Newman wrote the following song, "Lead Kindly Light":

I was not ever thus,
Nor prayed that thou should lead me on,
I loved to choose to see my path,
But now lead thou me on.

What a joy it is to know that there is hope for the foolish deeds of our past. Although we walked in the darkness of our past, we are now walking in the newness of life in the present. Bishop Charles Price Jones profoundly proclaimed this in his song, "I Will Make the Darkness Light":

> *I will make the darkness light before you,*
> *What is wrong I'll make it right before you,*
> *All thy battles I will fight before you,*
> *And the high place I'll bring down.*

Our wise choices make the lives and hearts of many glad. Just imagine how we cause the heart of God to rejoice with great jubilation each time we do unto others as we would have them do unto us. We cause the angels and the heavenly hosts to rejoice each time we bring a new soul into the kingdom of God, as well as each time we restore someone who has lost his or her way. Therefore, it is important that we not get weary in our well doing, for we should encourage ourselves to sow wise seeds today, and be assured of an abundance of endless blessings.

35

Your Integrity Is Priceless

A good name is better than riches.
Proverbs 22:1

Your integrity is the window of your soul. To know who you are is very important; who people think you are is also important. We should live the kind of lifestyle that reflects the character that honors God most. Good character will yield endless dividends as we go through life. The Bible points out that even a child is known by his deeds (Proverbs 20:11).

Many job applications require a character reference. Good character pays great dividends, both personally and interpersonally. Jesus, while teaching His disciples on the Mount of Olive in the book of Matthew, encouraged them to let their lights so shine that all may see their good works and glorify their Father which is in heaven. We should unselfishly want to be good and do good for God and for goodness' sake.

When we are good people, we reflect who God is. God is a good God, and in all of our ways, we should seek to let goodness and mercy follow us all of the days of our lives. The price we pay to do the right things in life has endless rewards. Some of the greatest of these rewards are not tangible. The supernatural rewards of peace and joy that accompany a good life surpass the price of silver and gold.

Integrity builds good character and total self-respect. Let us always remember that as good people we must bear good fruit. Good morality is mandatory to God's people. We are known by the fruit that we bear. We don't gather apples from a pear tree. Neither do we gather good fruit from corrupt trees. I am so grateful that God has many good trees bearing good fruit of all ages and all walks of life. In Psalm 1:30, David referred to these trees as trees that are planted by the water that brings forth its fruit in its season (Psalm 1:30).

I am convinced that all human beings are good-fruit potential. We were all created in the image of God. None of us was born to be corrupt or have unfruitful vines. Even after man fell in the garden of Eden, God had another plan, that His chosen people would be restored and bear fruit through Jesus Christ.

We should not attempt to do good or be good people merely to bring attention to ourselves or to feed our egos. We should always do good deeds with wholesome motives, and it will yield like consequences. We deceive ourselves if our motives are not honorable. We should not have ulterior motives, as did some of the religious people of Jesus' day. He warns that when we do good, we should not be as the phony religious leaders, as when He walked on earth. He mentions that they prayed and offered vain reputation to be seen and heard by men. He advises that we should never selfishly seek praise or attention for what we do.

As a schoolteacher, I encouraged my students to take pleasure in the great benefits of always doing the right thing, which is rewarding in itself. When parents and teachers refrain from promoting good behavior, children miss out on knowing the integrity of self-discipline.

God created us to have the option to choose self-will. He has given us the choice to choose between good and evil. We should teach our children early about the consequences of making bad choices. We should warn them of the terrible consequences of forbidden behavior. Moral integrity is a reward in itself.

Our greatest way of teaching others is through precepts and example. Action is greater than lip service. Even a child is known by his doing. None of us have done everything in the most perfect way. At some time, we have missed the mark of doing everything we should. Every day, we need His mercy and grace, but we should not abuse God's precious gift of grace. Grace promotes us to do what is pleasing to God. It is not our God-given consent to live immorally without terrible consequences.

When the Apostle Paul wrote to his son in the gospel of Titus, he admonished him to promote grace that teaches all of us to live soberly, righteously, and godly in this present world. The grace of God motivates us to demonstrate God's miraculous power. This miraculous power transfers us from the lifestyles of sin and corruption to become new creatures. We have been washed in the precious blood of Jesus, that we may live a victorious life. Not only will this new life bring us a good name, but it will bring us goodness and mercy that will follow us all the days of our lives, and we shall live in the Lord forever.

36

The Fullness of God's Love

God is love.

1 John 4:8

Love is God's greatest gift to mankind. Without love, life would be empty and meaningless. God so loved the whole world that He gave us His only Son, who gave us the source of abundant life. From the time of our birth and throughout adulthood, the need to be loved is a natural human craving.

Agape is God's love in supernatural action. God's love is the force in nature and the spiritual realm of life that uniquely sustains all of us. God's love is omnipotent, which means that He has almighty power to do everything and absolutely anything except fail. He is infinite in all His abilities. His love is omnipresent, meaning that He is capable of being present everywhere at one time. His love is omniscient, which means He is all-knowing. God's love is the fulfillment of all that we need or could ever ask or think. The hymn writer Fredrick M. Lehman so eloquently described this love in the song "The Love of God":

> *The love of God,*
> *The love of God is great.*
> *For the tongue or pen could never tell,*
> *It goes beyond the highest star,*
> *And reaches to the lowest hell.*
> *Oh love of God,*
> *How rich and pure,*
> *How measureless and strong.*
> *It shall forever more endure,*
> *The saint and angel's song.*

The true meaning of love is often universally misconceived in its definition. Love is of God. We cannot know the real or true definition of love until we experience who God is. God is a spirit, and love is spiritual. Human love is at its best when it is controlled or influenced by this love.

Eros, which is romantic love, is special. It is a gift from God. It was intended to be expressed at its best through the institution of marriage, as explained in Genesis

2:22–24. "Therefore, should a man leave his mother and father to cleave to his wife. She is bone of his bone and flesh of his flesh." Jesus advised husbands to love their wives as Christ loved the church. This love was divinely planned by God to be experienced only between a man and a woman. Romantic love was also divinely created to reproduce human life on the earth from generation to generation.

The third kind of love is known as phileo, which is humanitarian love. Humanitarian love is genuine love for all humankind. It is mandatory that this kind of brotherly love continue.

The greatest gift of God's love is the blessing of everlasting life. This is why we should respect all facets of human life, from conception to the grave. God told Adam and Eve to multiply and replenish the earth with life through procreation of their seed. Children are an inheritance unto the Lord. They are blessings for future generations.

The fullness of God is expressed in succession from one generation to another. His love is revealed most perfectly through His Son, Jesus, as recorded in Ephesians 3:17–20: "May Christ dwell in your hearts by faith, that you may be rooted and grounded in love. And that you may comprehend with all the saints the breadth, length, depth, and height to know the love of Christ, which passes human knowledge that you might be filled with the fullness of God."

I have made much reference in this chapter to the Word of God because the love of God and His Word are inseparable. God is His Word. Yes, God's love is expressed from Genesis to Revelation. The entire Bible is the greatest love story that has ever been told. "Behold what manner of love that God has bestowed upon us that we should be called the children of God" (1 John 3:1).

God's love is activated when we respond to love with love. He clearly states, "If you love me, you will keep my commandments" (John 15:10). The greatest commandment is that we love Him with all of our being and love all humanity as we love ourselves. God's love totally fulfills His plan for all of us so that we may experience the abundant blessings of life. The renowned love chapter of 1 Corinthians 13 very clearly explains the agape experience of love:

Love suffers long.
Love is kind.
Love is unselfish.
Love is slow to anger.
Love thinks no evil.
Love beareth, believeth, hopeth, and endureth all things.
And love never fails!

Divine love is everlasting. Nothing will ever be able to change God's love for His people. The question was asked, "Who shall separate us from the love of God?" (Romans 8:35). This age-old question was very profoundly answered by the great Apostle Paul in Romans 8:38-39. "For I am persuaded that neither death nor life, nor angels or principalities, nor powers or things present, nor things to come, neither height nor depth, or any other thing shall be able to separate me from the love of Christ, our Lord." To know the fullness of love is to know the fullness of God. It is God's will that we experience a taste of His heavenly blessings while we are yet residents here on the earth. This is an eternal process. This is the perfect will of God for all of us.

37

A Lot of Living to Do

I came that you may live life abundantly.
John 10:10

Life is the most precious gift that God has ever given to us. Life was meant by God, from the beginning, to be an everlasting experience of the best that He has to offer mankind. In the beginning, our perfect state of being was awesome, until the great fall of Adam and Eve. Life was beautiful. Life was excellent. And life was perfect.

Since the original fall in the garden of Eden, the quality of life has been altered tremendously. However, we now have access to living life to its fullest measure. The success of one's life depends upon how each person decides to live it. As the old folks often say, "Your life is what you make of it." How well we live is more important than how long we live.

I am often amazed by all of the great accomplishments of Dr. Martin Luther King Jr. Although his life span was only thirty-nine years, his accomplishments were enormous during this limited time. The quality of his life compensated for the short numbers of years of his life. Life on earth is short, even if one lives to be one hundred years old. Redeem the time. Never procrastinate doing those things that are important. Love, laugh, and live each moment with passion.

One of the greatest ways to multiply the quality of your life is to celebrate the lives of others. Let the joy of others be added to your joy. Allow the accomplishments of others to be as your own, and rejoice with them. Celebrate the possibilities of others as if they have already become everything that God expects them to be. Choose never to be envious or jealous of anyone. See yourself as an important part of others. You will find fulfillment in celebrating the success of others. Together, we can all look at each other and see the hope of overcoming our personal sorrows and disappointments by sharing the joy of others. In doing so, we can all perceive others as a part of our gigantic success story!

Parenting is awesome. Michelle and I are happy that we took the time to love each of our children uniquely. I am sure that all good parents feel there is always something more they can do to help their children.

Regardless of how much you have done, you want to do more. We enjoyed our children when they were small, and we enjoy them even now as adults.

Good children always find a way to show how they appreciate their parents. Parents who love each other make the best parents, because then they are better able to love their children. Good relationships between mothers and fathers create a wholesome and happy home environment that is mandatory in successfully raising children.

I am so grateful that I did not live my childhood and youthful days foolishly, with haste. Now that I look back over my life, I don't regret my abstinence from the worldly ways of seeking pleasure. I am very sensitive to my strong desire to never sound proud, self-righteous, or pious, but I am convinced that our young people need role models to show them that it can be done.

Life is too precious to spend it living carelessly and foolishly. There are too many good opportunities that can be missed by living life lethargically. Even with all of the problems that life may bring, life is wonderful. Again, I must say that life is as good as we live it.

Job said, "A man that is born of a woman is of few days and full of trouble" (Job 14:1). These troubles do not have to dominate our lives. They can be the wind beneath our wings when we choose to utilize the negatives in life to strengthen us. There is a cliché that I find amusing that says, "Take the lemons of life and make lemonade." This is good advice. However, don't forget to sweeten the lemonade with the honey and sugar experiences of life.

We should take examples from those who have gone before us and those who yet remain, who have very vividly demonstrated how we can wisely overcome all adversity. God has allowed me to observe examples, both male and female, both old and young, of diverse backgrounds to encourage me to take a stand and keep standing for righteousness and goodwill. There are times when this has been very trying in all of our lives, but we can do all things through Jesus Christ, our strength.

The choice of living the abundant and blessed life requires daily prayer, fortitude, and diligence. At every age, life presents new challenges. At sixty-three years old, I am now faced with new joy. My precious little granddaughter, Eleanor Grace, brings me joy that surpasses words. With this joy, I also accept the responsibility of being the best grandfather that I can be. I want to be sure that I do all that God expects me to do for her, as well as all of my future generations. I am convinced that, with God's help, this desire of my heart shall be successfully and completely fulfilled.

Michelle and I love to make our children and granddaughter happy. We enjoy the lovely pictures that our daughter, Hannah, often sends us. Knowing that Ellie enjoys the toys and other things that we do to make her happy makes us happy.

In facing the uncertainties of life, we can be filled with the certainty and blessed assurance that our best is yet to come. When we stand on the promise of God's Word, we are assured that He shall daily load us with His blessed benefits. Life will grow sweeter each day, as we are convinced that He will supply all of our needs, according to His riches (Philippians 4:19).

The unlimited life will extend itself beyond our natural life span here on earth. It moves to that eternal realm, where we will experience supernatural, everlasting joy and ecstasy with our loving Lord through His Son Jesus Christ. The renowned Evangelist Billy Graham so profoundly described this eternal state of perfect completeness and joy when he said, "One day, someone will tell you that Billy Graham is dead, but don't you believe a word of it, because I will be more alive than I've ever been in the presence of my loving Lord forever."

Arise now, and live life without limits every day, every hour, and every moment, now and forever more!

Special Memorial Tribute to My Father

Just as I was finalizing the manuscript of this book to be sent for publication, Daddy went home to be with the Lord. He lived a life that was an excellent example of the essence of this book. His life was one that exemplified the unlimited life. He lived and he died with dignity, honor, and integrity. His home-going service was as stately as a king's. We gave him the best of everything that would contribute to his first-class departure.

The massive crowd included clergy from numerous religious backgrounds. The acts of kindness and condolences were expressed by the mayors of Jackson, Mississippi, and Davenport, Iowa. There were special tributes from the Lieutenant Governor of Mississippi, city council members, senators, and many other community leaders. There was also representation from many civic and religious groups and also a host of friends and family from far and near.

The highlight of the service consisted of accolades

and tributes from Daddy's children and grandchildren. Momma demonstrated supernatural strength that counteracted the grief that we could have experienced. She wanted to remember him with special sentiments of their seventy-five wonderful years as husband and wife. She was consoled by how he had lived to see his one hundredth year and the experience and joy of successfully rearing their twelve children together. Amazingly, my giving Daddy's eulogy was the easiest I've ever given. The atmosphere was full of celebration, powerful praise, and divine joy.

Works Cited

"Congregation Rejoices as New Temple Opens." *Quad City Times*, July 26, 2001.

Dungy, Tony. *Quiet Strength: The Principles, Practices, and Priorities of a Winning Life.* Carol Stream: Tyndale House, 2007. Dung's memoir was released on July 10, 2007, and reached number one on the hardcover nonfiction section of the *New York Times* bestseller list on August 5, 2007, and again on September 9, 2007.

Johns Hopkins University. *The Johns Hopkins Family Health Book.* New York: Harper Collins Publishers, 1998.

King, Martin Luther, Jr. "I Have a Dream." Speech delivered on August 28, 1963.

Maya Angelou (1928–): Renowned, best-selling author, poet, historian, actress, playwright, civil rights activist, producer, and director.